Love and Other Passions

Poets of Central Florida

"With me poetry has not been a purpose, but a passion."

~ Edgar Allan Poe

Love
&
Other Passions

Poets of Central Florida

A Contemporary Anthology
Volume Two

Editors
BJ Alligood
Russ Golata
Gary Broughman

CHB Media
Publisher

ISBN 978-0-9851507-0-9

Library of Congress Control Number: 2012933194

CHB Media, Publisher
3039 Needle Palm Drive
Edgewater FL 32141
(386) 690-9295
CHBmedia@gmail.com

www.chbmediaonline.com

First Edition
Printed in the USA

The Poets

INTRODUCTION

In December of 2009 CHB Media joined with several of Central Florida's active poetry groups to publish *Poetry to Feed the Spirit, Poets of Central Florida*. The 122-page volume was an instant success. More than two years later poets and poetry fans are still talking about it.

We are proud to follow that triumph with *Love and Other Passions*, the second volume of *Poets of Central Florida*. This one is bigger and better. Almost sixty poets from around Central Florida are included. Poets from as far north as Gainesville and as far south as Merritt Island are represented. Of course, many poets from the greater Orlando area can be found on these pages, along with practitioners from up and down the Atlantic coast. Many poets in this contemporary anthology are active performers in groups like the First Monday Poets led by Russ Golata, one of the editors of this volume. BJ Alligood of the Tomoka Poets, who hosts the third Tuesday open mic group in Port Orange, also did wonderful work in selecting the best of the best from the hundreds of submissions we received.

Many, perhaps most, of the poets we chose have been published in magazines, journals, anthologies, and in their own poetry books. Others have been "closet" poets who are finally letting their work see the light of day. What all of them have in common is their dedication to craft. If you enjoy good poetry, I ask you to read just one poem; you'll have a hard time putting the book down.

Finally, my thanks to poets everywhere who combine heart and mind to breathe spirit into our lives. In my view, creativity is the highest order of human endeavor, and when it comes to the written arts, poetry stands on the summit.

Gary Broughman
CHB Media

"Poetry is finer and more philosophical than history, for poetry expresses the universal, and history only the particular."
~ Aristotle

Al Hubbs

Al Hubbs makes his home in Orlando. He lives a life that many might envy: an actor in film, television and stage, stand-up comedian, radio DJ, announcer, teacher, script writer, poet and photographer. His creative works includes two books of poetry, a book of short stories and a text on the craft of film acting.

WHERE YOU ARE

I've seen the world through
                    a wanderer's eyes
Watched Northern Lights in Canadian skies
Stood on a mountain in old Cathay
    And dined in Patagonia
                    at the end of day

No matter where I went
                    this much I knew
The roads I followed led me to you

Felt the restless wind so cold and strong
    Where the Antarctic nights
                    were dark and long
New York sidewalks to Chicago towers
Hong Kong gardens and Hawaiian flowers

    But through it all
                    one thought is true
The face I always dreamed was you

But here where all the mangroves grow
And those soft tropical
                    breezes blow
Like the mariner who follows his star
    Where I am is where you are

THE PARTING

The old house stands empty: rooms and
walls are bare
Only a few dust motes hang in the musty
air
She promised to return or so the story
goes
Why that never happened nobody really
knows
His knock upon the door sent trembling
flying
How often had he heard those same
echoes dying?
"I loved you" he cried out." Why did you
go away?"
His call merely stirred up the ghosts of
yesterday
"Tell her I came," he said, "and that I kept
my word"
He was never certain that anybody heard
The long years gathered as the decades
came and went
His stature once so tall became quite frail
and bent
All that's left is silence where once his
footsteps fell
In that endless quiet you can hear the
parting knell
The old house stands empty: there's no one
there to care
Only a few dust motes hang in the musty
air

ONE, TWO, THREE

One
great love
In a magical moment
When the universe
is aligned

Two
trusting hearts
Forever joined together
Just as nature
has designed

Three
little words
Filled with adoration
That's how my love
is defined

Alea Plumley

Alea Plumley has been writing poetry since her early teens and has been a free-lance artist for some thirty years. A published children's book illustrator, Alea has completed several novels. Designing greeting cards, painting murals, acting and ballroom dancing are a few of the ways she expresses her creative energy. Alea has lived in Florida for the past twenty-five years.

IN MY DREAMS

In my dreams I live in vivid colors
My soul rises and flies
With my body not far behind
I glide dance with the butterflies
Voice harmonizing with the winds

I am a gifted artist
Creating my life with watercolors
The rains may come
Colors blend and wash away
I will paint a new life

I hear with my heart
I know the riches of your soul
Pleasure sharing with another's spirit
I have uncovered many treasures
I have no complaints

I created colors so alive
I felt them with my eyes
Seen love in someone's touch
Allowing my soul to dance
Life is a wonderful chance

Felt the softness of a kittens fur
That filled my ears
My dreams would amaze you
For they are not dreams at all
Only my canvas, my paints... my life

CREATIVE PASSIONS

Poets need a place to Poe
To unfold words they long to sew
Expressing their words on the page
Edgar Alan, of course, was an old sage

Comedians create with Whit, man
Causing laughter as the plan
Not shy, they love the attention
Walt, of course, was to humble to mention

Cooks love their meat a Browning
Rare on the inside, in gravy are drowning
In their kitchen they are the king
Robert, of course, wrote about spring

Teachers teachings are very Thoreau
Giving children all they know
Wisdom bestowed within their minds
Henry David, of course, expressed treasures of kinds

Musicians play music they Long to fellow
Classical or jazz that's smooth and mellow
Hearing them play their melodic tunes
Henry Wadsworth, of course, offered us moons

Families create in loving Holmes
Beauty and blessings protected by gnomes
With a joyous heart there is love to spare
Oliver, of course, penned with flair

Passion comes in numerous forms
Sharing your gift beyond the norms
The pleasure of loving the talent you're given
Each of us, of course, is respectfully driven

INSPIRATION

Blessings untold for souls to see
Love embracing their every need
Touched by the dreams we ner' express
Meadows await mornings' echo

Charismatic desires unfathomed
Exhaling forth from resonant heartbeat
The urgency is superior to ourselves
Sun rests light on prismatic splendor

Progressing with vital energy
Written on thin stale parchment
Denial of overtures forgotten
Calm oceans acquiesce to frothed eruption

Silently seeping over structured lies
Artistic spirit captivating quiet muse
Fusing exquisite gracefulness and resistant edges
Inspired sky bestows light across amused clouds

Movement's influence will not cease
Invading spirit articulates creation's rhythm
Uniting steps that remain unclaimed
Earth dances elegantly the universal ballet

Barbara Fifield

Barbara Fifield is a retired social worker and journalist who has published widely in newspapers and literary journals. She is the author of two novels, *Photographs and Memories* and *Lucifer Rising*, and a book of poetry, *Passion's Evidence*. Barbara is a member of several writing groups, and the Florida Writers Association. She resides in Port Orange, Florida.

PICKING STRAWBERRIES

Moving right to left
    row on row,
        I am picking strawberries,
            blushing rubies of succulent flesh,
                food for ancient deities.

Early men knew no passion from other fruits
    or their souls in lust be consumed.

Gnashing incisors into this June dessert,
    my saliva blends into rosy juices.
    I taste the first rush of summer.
    It pounds on my skin and hair.
    Wind-swept grass crawling into poison ivy
    Blue bells, hyacinths and daffodils nudging my legs –
        fields where strawberries bend and sag.

My fingers drool scarlet like a wine maker's.
    Passion's evidence-
        eating strawberries
            too succulent and sweet for summer.

I let juices run down my fingers
    and knees in crimson worms,
        sticky streams hard to wash off.
        Don't rub them off.
            It isn't time.

As I Look into Your Eyes

Looking into your eyes-
   dark and somber, solid,
I feel the passion
   of my love for him.
Did you also swim along his side?
Did you slam a ball across the court
   and have him swing it back again?

And feel the directness of his eyes.
    and know that he loved you, too.
Your gaze slides away from mine.
   as if regretting its betrayal.
But my heart skips,
   knowing your secret.
I have lost too much to let go.
   Bring him back with your story eyes.

CATCHING FIREFLIES

Fluttering her wings against my dark veins
I hesitate to let go
Summer's almost gone
There aren't many of these.

Soon autumn gusts will scare away what remain
No more to catch
I must hold on while I can.

I reminisce about childhood barbecues,
Children playing hide 'n' seek,
Mothers comforting babes,
Girls' giggles as they first light up.
There's a freedom and impermanence about them.
Like fireflies,
They flicker for a second before dying out.

The bug stretches out her legs
She spins between my fingers
Off into the darkness
To join others before a quick demise.
She takes her freedom –
The last spark of hope.

Brian Morse

Brian Morse is the founder of the band Treblehawk, an all original music band out of Ocala, Florida. He has been working with words and music for most of his life and tours and performs often at festivals and venues with his band. Much of his poetry is geared to be more lyrical though he does sometimes write prose-etic.

I AM ONE

I am one I see the future
I know I'm flawed in this human form
And who I am is not who I'll be
I know my days Will be calm and storm

We are two we stand together
And If you fall just lean on me
We share our love and our heartache
You are the one that comforts me

We are three we are complete
She gave us all yet asked for none
And she's the one we hope to be
We lay together in the morning sun

We are two we mourn her passing
Within our hearts remains the hole
It won't be filled it's always bleeding
There's two of us yet we feel alone

Now I am one I see the future
To die alone with just my memories
When I see you both on the other side
We will rejoice and forever be

BE THE CHANGE

Wisdom's not decided by your social position
Beauty's never had a specific definition
Never trust an act based solely on tradition
Fighting for your rights is not an act of sedition
People everywhere are dying to be free
It's gonna take some work to make it reality
You got to make the world what you want it to be
You got to be the change that you want to see

 All around the world they are questioning the schism
Bailing out a bank is also socialism
Questioning your government is an act of patriotism
Give me some antiestablishmentarianism
People everywhere are dying to be free
It's gonna take some work to make it reality
You got to make the world what you want it to be
You got to be the change that you want to see

Tommy said we're born with freedom from oppression
And each can chase their happiness at their own disgression
But their are those who profit through buying more
repression
Washington is taking bids and congress is in session
People everywhere are dying to be free
It's gonna take some work to make it reality
You got to make the world what you want it to be
You got to be the change that you want to see

That Stupid Irish Love Song
Words & Music

It's another night alone
In my quiet and exile home
And I think about the night I fell in love
You were standing in the yard
As I drove up in my car
And You smiled at me like a goddess from above

And you walked right up to me
With no shoes upon your feet
And you kissed me for the first time of the night
And I knew right then and there
The this girl with the golden hair
Was the woman I had searched for all my life

And now that your gone I can see where I went wrong
My sorrow is a river from my eyes
There is one remaining truth
I am still in love with you
And I will be 'till the stars no longer shine

We made love that moonlit night
For the very first time
And I watched you sleeping sweetly in my arms
And I gently touched your face
As I prayed I was awake
And not dreaming as I surrendered to my heart

And I think what hurts the most is that you may never know
The love I have for you deep inside
There is one remaining truth
I am still in love with you
And I will be 'till the stars no longer shine

Yes I know I've made mistakes t'was me that pushed you
'way
Now I wish you all the happiness you may find
There is one remaining truth
I am still in love with you
And I will be 'till the stars no longer shine
Yes I will be 'til the stars no longer shine

Catherine Giordano

Catherine Giordano is president of TalksAllAbout.com, a company devoted to writing and public speaking. She has published a book of poetry, *The Poetry Connection*, and a book of essays based on her speeches, What Ifs, If Onlys, and So Whats. She lives in Orlando.

Forgotten Words

I don't recall
My mother ever telling me
"I love you."

I think she loved me.
But she never said it.

When I raised my son,
I said "I love you" twenty times a day.

But when he became an adult,
The "I love you's" faded away.

I still love him as much as ever,
But I don't say it.

Why not?
Is it just a habit
That has fallen away?

Sometimes my son speaks to me on the phone,
He ends the conversation with "I love you."
Is he trying to tell me he still needs to hear it?

Of course I love you!
I do everything for you!

But I don't say it.
And he needs to hear it.

I will tell him today.

FALLING IN LOVE

Falling in love is like driving a car
Sometimes I take it slow
Careful
Cautious
I obey all the rules of the road
Until I arrive at a dead end.

Other times, I press the accelerator to the floor
It's like I'm drunk
Careening down the road
Flying through stop signs
It is so exciting
Until I crash.

I leave my car in the garage these days.
It's safer that way.

OLD WITCHES NEVER DIE

Ding Dong, the wicked witch is dead!
So there's nothing more to be said?
Except this statement does belie
the fact that
we know old witches never die.

They are like an undead monster—
Despite it all, they live forever.
They stay out of sight, well hidden,
until they
can lurch to life unbidden.

There is a witch who is named Fear.
She's always present, always near.
Her spell, her dire consequence,
is that she
cruelly erodes your confidence.

Another witch is the one called Hate.
How she mangles and maims your fate!
She is burrowed deep in your heart
just waiting,
to pounce and tear your life apart.

Let's not forget the one called Rage.
She looses anger from its cage.
She steals calm and brings disquiet,
when she does
suddenly bring forth a riot.

Then there's the twins, one called Envy,
The other is known as Jealousy.
They gnaw at your guts, this soulless pair,
and when done
they spit them out and disgorge despair.

Another witch, her name is Sadness—
She brings her own kind of badness.
The doldrums, the dumps, depression
is her way
of blighting joy and expression.

One last foul sister, call her Shame.
We hang our head and take on blame.
She creeps up and spews her poison
leaving you
feeling worthless, failed, and undone.

We can choose, and we can decide!
We can commit a witch-a-cide!
We choose happiness and the light,
and we can
cast out the demons of the night.

We can stand against them, bar the door.
Banish them to some distant shore.
Caldron boil and cauldron bubble,
no longer
can they etch your soul with trouble.

George Bishop

George Bishop is the author of four chapbooks, most recently the forthcoming *Old Machinery* to be published at White Violet Press. Others include *Love Scenes, Marriage Vows and Other Lies.* Recent work has appeared in Pirene's Fountain, Obsession and Medulla Review. Bishop attended Rutgers University and now lives and writes in Kissimmee, Florida.

THINKING OF YOU FROM A CANOE
for C.F.

Paddling Shingle Creek,
the banks of southern oaks
and cedar tipping my mind
toward the next bend, a tinge
of prehistoric silence is still
in the air, a vestige of crude
instinct foraging the underbrush,
a banished lover with a plan.
The nakedness of each
unseen eye holds fast
against my intrusion,
each behind a veil
of deception designed
by some endless network
of light and dark.
The otter alters between
a world of air and one of water,
the woodpecker works from dead
tree to dead tree—diversions all.
I sink into the brackish arena
afraid to look back, to look down,
struggling with the drapes
of Spanish moss.

Almost Home

Nothing except the sounds of the house—
clocks at work clearing their throats,

always behind, half a cup of coffee
still awake, staining what we left

unsaid and certain kitchen air hiding
deep in the face of a spoon.

The cat wants something or nothing
and a fly in the window's stunned

by what's not in the window. Maybe
I'm just looking too far ahead,

undressing what's coming up the stairs
after hearing a secret knock at every door,

undressing as it comes—there's bound to be
something missing after it finds me.

After all, I've been here the whole time,
straightening the picture of my mother

while the picture of my father straightens
a picture of me. I'm thinking I should

write to my sister, the other only child
who's listening from another room, pivoting.

It's been a long time since we've all
been this close. Almost home.

TOAST

I've always insisted a toast
be performed with just one glass
ever since my divorce came together—

you know, that sensation of, say,
a bus drifting back, your mind
still moving forward, body at ease

until the departure stuns the eye,
tricks you. That's what falling
out of love feels like someone once

told me. Yes, one glass. No
ting of temporary goodwill,
no collision of separate crystal,

just some sweet breath pulling
the wine past a pair of lips,
one lover at a time—

you making sure to drink last,
someone else wondering
if you've taken too much

and both breaking other glasses
against two new beds
of rekindled coal.

Dave Bennett

Dave holds a BA in art and speech/theatre, a NHA in nursing home administration, and an MFA in theatrical design from Ohio University. He has been a public school teacher and high school wrestling coach, a nursing home administrator and a professional costume and scenic designer. Currently he is working in costume management in the theme park industry.

XVI

I just spent four days
in a cabin in the mountains.

It's amazing how many
hundreds of thousands
of acres of this beautiful
planet are still yet covered
with trees, bushes, wild
flowers, rocks and water.

Man has cleared only just
enough space to be able
to enjoy the grandeur
of all that remains.

You are like those mountains;
tall, majestic, beautiful and
still somewhat wild and untamed.

Only a narrow path has been cleared
thru that strong exterior.

XIV

You don't send me flowers any more.
You sang that to me...
as we passed one another
along the trail.

You were with your new love.

You were carrying a bouquet
of wild flowers.

At first I thought
it was just
a coincidence,
even though it hurt.

I would still be sending
you flowers
if
we were still together!

Now, days later,
I'm haunted by the image
of you...passing me...
the warm rays of the sun
shining on your face...
the bouquet of wild flowers
in your hands...
your voice singing quietly
those words.

Would I be hoping too much
to think you were trying
to send me a message?

You love me, you love me not.
You love me, you love me not.
You love me!

I continue to slash away at all
that has grown up around
you thru your years.

My only "blade"...
the point of my pen.

I grow weary,
but remain determined
to survive,
and,
someday reach my destination...
your heart.

X

The bloom has fallen
from your presence
without ever having fully
developed.

The leaves have grown weak
and discolored;
only two remain.

Yet, I continue to water
and nurture.

And when the final leaf
is gone,
I'll plant still another bulb
in your honor
and begin again
to cultivate
your love.

Someday we'll raise
a strong
healthy "blossom"
to celebrate
your freedom.

Your freedom
to love
and to be loved
by me.

Joan Hartwig

Joan Hartwig is an artist, photographer, novelist and poet who enjoyed a long career as a Professor of English Renaissance Literature. She taught at Florida State University and at the University of Kentucky, published two books on Shakespeare, essays on John Donne and Andrew Marvell, and is the author of the suspense novel *Alligator Pool*.

SAMSON, MY KITTEN

Samson was never meant to be my kitten.
I sought out his sister, but she died young.
When I went to get her, he was there,
Leader of the litter,
Having led them all to rescue.

He went toward my purse on the floor
When I went to meet his sister.
So I took them both.
How could I know how beloved he would become?
He is the light of my life.

Totally sweet, soft, and full of fleas that don't show up
Except when I comb him.
He is the total purpose of existence on some days.
He leads me forward,
Just as he did his litter.

I probably should have named him Moses.
But Samson seems so strong.
And he's never had his hair cut.

SOMETHING ABOUT ARTISTS

Artists are full of love.
It spills out in their paintings,
But is not captured there.
Friendships arise that
Surpass family relationships.

They understand when you feel down.
They care. And they give warmth.
Miles of undefined feeling are allowed,
Accepted, and understood.

Words are not hallowed, but allowed.
Something deeper happens.
We bond in a place
Not unlike heaven.

If we could define it,
We would not care to be there.

THE WATCH

My mother's watch stopped at the moment of impact.
The truck had swerved to avoid hitting the car.
That's why she almost died at 8:20 pm.
She lived, and I kept the watch.
Never tried to start it again or wear it.
It was, I thought, a tribute to her survival.
Today, at the watchmaker's, repairing my old watch,
I mentioned her watch, in better shape than mine.

A woman, who was selling her gold jewelry to survive, said,
"Of course, you may be superstitious. But I think
It would honor her to start the watch again and wear it."
I never thought of it that way.
I always wanted to keep the moment in stasis
When she saw God and lived.

Now, I see another view of time.

Joe Cavanaugh

A writer, poet and journalist from an early age, he authored his first book in 1972, His second book, "The Peace Dividend, Defense Conversion through Higher Education" was published by the Leon and Sylvia Panetta Institute in 2000. He is a past winner of a New York Times Writing Award, and is currently Treasurer of the Florida State Poets Association.

I Watched Your Hands Last Night

Your caress
deep
supple

Glistening satisfaction
intense complex
outpouring

To be new again
To renew again

Long languid fingers
of delight

Playing with me
Reaching inside me

Sounding the clear note
that is my destiny

A Wedding Poem For Joy And Bill

June 11, 2006

On this beautiful afternoon in June
Joy has married Bill
and Bill has married Joy

It's a sunny Sunday
blue sky and warm breeze
witness the pair
now bound together and allied
like voice and song
bee and flower
tree and bird
sage and honey
rain and shine
apple pie and ice cream

The lovers smile at each other
the bride unveiling herself
for the bridegroom

their personal discovery of intimacy
essentially belonging
to the source of everything

They fly up together
over the lush island of Kauai
to view the curve of the earth

here the sky is a dazzling blue
a long way from the weight of the earth
they soar into a sweet new dimension

Forever remembering
this sunny Sunday
when two became one   (*cont.*)

landing
she as goddess
he as white knight

May the evening star salute them
as their heart beats in rhythmic harmony
and their constellations combine in the heavens

UNEXPECTED JOY

A quiet walk with you
after the summer rain

HARP (Judith Brent)

Judith teaches at a small private college, usually freshman English, but also humanities, psychology, and other subjects. She has degrees in English (BS), Marriage & Family (MEd.), Addictions CAGS, Public Administration (MPA), Counselor Ed., ABD, (PhD). She says she would spend her days writing if it guaranteed a roof over my head and fresh groceries!

WHAT WAS HER NAME?

In venerable old world
Woodstock I knew a woman
Retired from too much peace,
Love, rock and roll
Who determined to pay
Attention to the world from
Her upstairs den of memories-
Know one saw through the second floor curtains' lace
To view the wizened still
Young face that answered
Questions about would be
Suitors of similar history
With another question –
"What do I need That for?-
She puttered about busily,
Collected social
Security and a few rental
Checks from wise green investments
When everyone else thought
No further than the next
Piece, loving, rock and roll.

Spy

Upstairs the neighbor has a
Tracking device,
It tells him when there is heat
And where it is,
...just like James Bond.

The neighbors ask about
One special person,
Knowing each other, anonymity
Scares them, they turn
Lovingly to one who spys,
....even if he is a little crazy.

In the downstairs apartment
Someone leaves for work,
An enigma each fourteen hour day,
Welcome grieving each night,
Silent calm from months of pain
Not worth speaking about,
Except to Mother universe.

Upstairs the neighbor watches the
Heat seeking dot move and walks
To each new position;
Downstairs says aloud,
"Get a life of your own."

Healthy Aging

A youngish twenty-five
Flash frozen by a
Divorced soul mate back when
I thought sparing another diagnosed and indeterminate
Life realities meant love,
Before daily wear
Taught me about trust,
Faith, tenacity,
True love.

Saw myself forty years hence,
In a self-sufficient of my
Wooded home simply riding her
Harley to a one gas pump
Outpost, for plasticized milk
Perhaps peanut butter, stuffed
In fatigue-green backpack.

Then creased, worn
Leather jacket and matching face turned
From my open admiration, swung
A still-nimble leg over beautiful
Hair.

I am still becoming the her my eye appreciated,
Youngish, beyond birthdays,the open road
Beckons my solid two thousand pound wheels
While I search out another
Less devastating soulmate than
The latest, admire the constant pines
outside my door, create my
own peanut butter, stay nimble.   (*cont.*)

Hair unsheared into easy care
Pseudo-masculine ideal, mostly
I aspire to a rear view as
Captivating; that memory of
Glowing locks tamed into
A thick silver braid whose
Smiling curls tickled a taut waist.

Leslie C. Halpern

Leslie Halpern's poetry has appeared in publications including *Poetry to Feed the Spirit, Connections: A Collection of Poems, Windows to the World, A Poet's Haggadah,* and *SciFaiKuest.* She authored three nonfiction books, including *Reel Romance,* and *Dreams on Film.* Website: http://home.roadrunner.com/~lesliehalpern

AFTERNOON ILLUMINATION

Riding to a late lunch at his favorite Mexican grille,
he halfheartedly considers pre-calculus homework.
Bright sunlight reflects off pavement into our eyes –
will the car plunge into dark depths of an asphalt sea?
I bravely speed through another Florida mirage.
Soon his book lies on gritty carpeted floor, still sandy
from a recent trip to New Smyrna Beach.

He brushes a curl from his forehead, rubs tight skin
between his brows.
"I can't concentrate," he says in his cracking adolescence,
"because sunlight glistening through this canopy of trees
disorients me like a strobe light at a party."
Someday my son will notice a girl surrounded by strobe light
as music's guise intentionally lures their young bodies
together.
She'll be familiar – exotic and enticing – yet safe like finally
coming home,
seducing him with her disorienting shadow dance.
I hope she doesn't embrace him too possessively
or crush his size elevens with her forceful stance.
That she also has a poet's soul, craves late afternoon
quesadillas.

SWEET SEDUCTION

From the crowded dessert tray
petit four politely begs my vote
teases my fingers, entices my lips
tempts my tongue, tickles my throat
soothes my stomach, taunts my hips
not with proud delightful decadence
but in a far more cunning way –
with smooth lies of its dainty innocence.

APPRAISAL

In a competitive market
with fluctuating cycles
of supply and demand,
scrutinized, itemized, magnified –
though not yet an antique –
value increased over time.
Rare, unusual, one of a kind;
preserved in a smoke-free home,
still in original package,
condition: very fine to excellent,
only slightly used; no missing parts.
All pieces remain intact
except, perhaps, my heart.

Lin Neiswender

Lin Neiswender has written creatively since childhood, when she was thrilled to see her first theme posted on the bulletin board at Parent's Night. She lives in Orlando, Florida, owned by a feisty cat and laid-back dog. Her poems and flash fictions stories have appeared online and in print.

LOVE'S PROGRESS
- A VILLANELLE -

Love takes wing and flies away
Shy Cupid with arrows adrift
Leaves mere mortals to seize the day

Blushing glances longings betray
Pulses beating now more swift
Love takes wing and flies away

Stem by stem a sweet bouquet
Rose and lilac scents do lift
Leaves mere mortals to seize the day

Soft low voices fears allay
Giving fear a mere short shrift
Love takes wing and flies away

New lover's whisper, a tender play
Hearts will meet then souls uplift
Leaves mere mortals to seize the day

One kiss may give passion sway
A final tender parting gift
Love takes wing and flies away
Leaves mere mortals to seize the day

Amoré, Zombie Style

How do I love thee?

Let my body count the ways.

Your warm embrace
Makes this zombie's heart race.
Baby, let's go eat some brains.

Your fingers may rot
But I'm still besot;
Smell of putrid flesh attracts me.

Your knees may wobble
But I still hobble
Toward you on one foot and a skateboard.

Your heart is still
Yet gives me a thrill
When I see it poking out your ribcage.

Your eye so bright,
Lost the other one last night
In a scuffle with a rival clan.

Your dragging arms
Another of your charms--
Come, gimme a kiss.

But I forget--no lips.

First printed in "Vicious Verses and Reanimated Rhymes: Zany Zombie Poetry for the Undead Head", 2009

CAT-CRAZIES LOVE

Leaping arc of kitty bounds
From doorway to my solar plexus
As I stretch out on the bed,
This declaration of your affection goes
Whoosh! as all air rushes from
 My lungs.

Your sinuous, love-filled frame
Twining around my ankles makes
Every paw-bitch-slapped step
More precious as I stumble down
The stairs.

Better yet, how well you express yourself
A rocket of cat blasting off from behind
The closed bathtub curtain, right past
My nose, as I sit on the toilet,
Scaring the shit out of me
Literally.

Still I admire the dainty way
You taunt the dog
Lapping smelly cat food just out of
His reach, so all he can do
Is haunt the cat box for
Tootsie Rolls.

And when the cat crazies are done,
We curl up on my winter bed to sleep,
Butt to butt, you my faithful little
Four-legged, space heater companion
Cozy and warm, dreaming of new ways
To sabotage me with your
Cat-crazies love.

Mary Jane Barenbaum

I started writing poetry and some prose about ten years ago. I have no formal training but have had very encouraging people advise me to "just keep going". I have been published in *East on Central Poetry and Arts* journals in 2006, 2007 and 2010 in Chicago. I was also published in 2009 in *Poetry to Feed the Spirit: Poets of Central Florida.*

My House

I want a house that shoots through the starry night
Bedecked with diamond shaped lights to lead the way
I want my starship to reach behind the moon
To nestle up to the evening blush of that bashful globe
I want a room with floating pillows enfolding my unruly past
Silken stairways reaching to my ghosts lingering for me
in the by and by
A riotous rose garden in the center of my flying mansion
with a feather bed to rest my bones
I will forgive my bygone deeds in the labyrinth
of scarlet petals.
My house will wrap gleaming neon arms around
tender shoulders
of all of us too weak to make it alone
I will soar to the heavens then back to earth
gathering my far flung dynasty for moments of joy
It may be in their early morning dreams of nonsensical play
with a feeling of pleasure too great to explain
 All, past and present will be in my vessel of
forgiveness and love
Each room ablaze with the sheer radiance of being

FRIDAYS WITH HEATHER

She's always late,
tires squealing into the parking lot

 A smile says, I'm here at last

Door flies open, wind playing a symphony
with mahogany hair,
reaching to the waist when captured

We rush to hug, letting giggles
escape our throats

Her tresses cover me like a silken cape

I watch with humor as patrons and
waiters gasp at her beauty

A valentine heart is jealous
of that glowing face

The Caribbean seems gray
in a contest with her eyes

We order our iced tea and cherry coke.
Keeps us going in our breathless talkathon

Subjects as light as the color
of her new eye shadow

As heavy as when the death of her mother
will become easier to carry

I want to wrap her in arms that are
bullet proof to pain, instead

I ask her when she is going dancing again

Does she have another tarot card gig?

Did she see any good movies?

Laughing and grabbing her hand
at the delightfully innocent answers

She wants to know if I feel OK

Did I write any poems this week?

Would I send her a copy?

We manage to eat between the
ping-pong of our words

It's time to leave and we walk to our cars,
shoulders touching

Next week, Grandma?

THE MAROON COAT

I remember the smell of the fur collar
on your maroon coat, cold on my cheeks,
and your dark curls, damp
from the unexpected snow.

I hugged you for dear life
I was like a puppy in those days.
When you left home, I thought it was forever.
There came a time I knew
you would not desert me.
What drowned the fear, I do not recall.

I remember you standing on one foot
as you pulled up your nylons.
You looked back over your shoulder
to check the black seams as they
traveled up your legs.

In the afternoon, I would lie on your bed
watching you at your dressing table.
You sat on an upholstered stool
brushing your wild curls
until your arm could take no more.
 A lit cigarette burned untouched
in an ashtray shaped like a half moon.
 You would reach for it and
inhale so deep the ashes turned
orange chasing down to your mouth.

I loved the way you pursed your lips
when you put on the deep red lipstick.
You smudged a little on your cheeks and glowed.
To this day I purse my lips the same.
I look in the mirror and I swear I see you.

I remember the sweet smell of your washed hair
as I gently combed out the tangles.

The black now winter gray, the thick waves limp to the
touch, scalp showing white in the afternoon light.

You loved for me to cut your hair and
make pin curls until it dried.

I remember laughing until I cried when
you had me put on your make up
for a rare outing to shop for shoes or to the doctor.

"Oh, too much" you squealed

"Not enough" I giggled back.

I remember how small you had become,
a little child in a women's body.
I could carry you from place to place.
You never spoke of the killing disease that
gripped your breath. You longed each day,
each hour for one more cigarette.

I couldn't know when the last day would be.
I didn't plan for it. It was just that day.
That day it happened.

And no day after was the same.

Mary Susan Clemons

Mary Susan Clemons lives in Edgewater, Florida. She is an active member of a local poetry group, The Poet's Corner Workshop, and is a part-time moderator at Wild Poetry Forum, an on-line poetry workshop site. Please Google, Mary Susan Clemons, if you would like to read more of her work.

THE HUMANE SOCIETY

The family voices breach the door.
With a slide-click, the other world steps in.
The beagle bays.
The trained German Shepard
sits, waits for "Heal."
I stayed folded, my back to the barred door.
Yips and barks mark their approach.
The man reads my card.

Breed – nothing special
Age – too old to break bad habits
Reason – why did my loved one abandon me?

The children race on.
The man follows.
But the woman stays. I glance at her.
She squats, her voice encouragement.
I open up and stand. She smiles.
My tail beats waltz time between my legs.
I ease toward her 'til fingers touch snout.

Memories.
A sun warmed couch. Feet snug against
my side. A home to defend. Love to protect.

The children beg, "Momma, come see."
The woman moves out of vision.
Cold settles where her fingers had warmed.

MY HUSBAND, YOU ARE HOME

I sit on the couch's curb,
my jaw set on control.
The tears are burned from my eyes,
and my mind filters the pain.

Your urn's blue tiles, patterns of shades,
cool my fingertips,
inside the scrap metal slivers mix
among your ashes.

They have come, in their dress blues,
knowing that they exist only because of you,
to tell of the last six months of tent-living
and the reality of war, and to gather

tales of humor and pride
offered by family and friends
to make the essence of the man
living in their memory, real.

I watch them, picking the ripe stories of your life,
and would gladly trade anyone of them
to have you back.

I wish, just this once, you had been selfish.

Published Summer 2009 Strong Verse.com

Southern Potato Salad

You can find it in the Fellowship Hall
on the communion table, between
the macaroni salad with its diced bell peppers
and the thick slices of Georgia reds.

Or perhaps you tasted it when the hospital
became part of your daily routine
blended with family from Tennessee
and North Carolina. The Smiths
took Monday, Andersons Tuesday,
and Wednesday was Ruth King's make
your own subs and her secret family recipe.

You might have found it in the Kroger deli,
held it smashed against a plastic container,
recalled southern evenings on a pine cooled
porch balancing it on a Dixie plate.

Or was it at the annual June picnic
that you had your first taste. With or without
the brown skins, with or without Vidalia
onions, with or without mustard,
but always with the yellow and white of boiled
eggs and potatoes firm as the farmer's
hilled biceps; blended with mayonnaise
creamy as Sunday morning's sermon
with a celery crunch and a sweet relish twang.

Published Triggerfish Critical Review Issue 1

Oral Nussbaum

Born in Marshallville, Ohio, Oral now resides in Winter Springs, Florida. He is co-leader of a local writers group, and organizer of a monthly spiritual discussion group. He has been published in the *Dream Flight* newsletter in London, England, *Deaf Digest*, and *Velocity* magazine.

BURIED TREASURE

With sorrows laid
in shallow graves,
we run through our tomorrows
darting to and fro
in fear
they'll capture us again;
until we see
they were never ours,
never real,
and never even sorrows.

Dear sunlit moon,
cast your crystal light
upon these tombs
that we may know
what we have buried
is needed
for its opposite to be.

We are the Beauty
and the Beast,
the Jekyll
and the Hyde.
'Tis on these wings of paradox
we fly to freedoms door,
in hope that someone...
will let
both of us in.

EMOTIONAL GUIDE
(IS NOT AN OXYMORON)

What was I thinking?
That's easy to see.
I just look at the things
that are happening to me.

Where was my head?
That's not hard to find.
We create in our lives,
what we hold in our mind.

Why is this happening?
Just take a look.
The pen's in your hand,
you wrote your own book.

How do I make right,
all that is wrong?
Put down that sad hymnal,
stop singing that song.

We blame the devil,
bad luck and fate,
for the fruit on our trees
and the food on our plate.

But we planted that tree,
and cooked our own meal.
Life is not about destiny,
it's about how you feel.

We've been given a guide-post,
a shining North star
that shows us where we're going,
tells us where we are.

We've traveled eons of time
and now we're much nearer
to understanding our lives
as a big cosmic mirror,

Reflecting beliefs,
then thought and emotion.
The image *will change*
when we get the notion,

To follow our hearts
in all that we do.
Intuition, my friend,
is God talking to you!

Life's Palette

Whispers from my youth
like a misguided sculptor
have thusly
shaped my world.
Not by Almighty decree
nor commission
were these colors
splashed
on my canvass of life...
twas my hand
holding the brush
all along.

This truth
can drown me
in a pool of chastisement,
or liberate me
from a gallery of pain,
to paint a new story
and mould new beginnings,
from which
tomorrow is born.

Rachael Salter

Rachael Salter grew up in Fort Lauderdale, Florida. After high school she attended college in Orlando, Florida, which she now calls home. Her love for writing began at the age of fourteen as a release from the adversities of life. Today, her writing continues to evolve, as her inspiration comes directly from her soul and through life experiences.

SUPERNOVA

I am showered in meteors.
Hot masses
trickle down my spine.
Tingling
as they collide onto my skin.
I am wrapped in a blanket
of nebulas
to keep warm.
I fell asleep next to the moon last night.
Woke up this morning
Shimmering
in the sun.
It's hard to keep
your balance
when the tide comes in.
One must be
Careful
not to fall.

WHAT YOU SHOULD TEACH YOUR DAUGHTERS

God created woman with Adam's rib.
And it's the closest they'll ever get to a man's heart.
For centuries, women have longed to find their one true love
as if such a thing even exists.
Teach your daughters to stop searching for 'the one'
and start searching for themselves.

They say that a child's mind is that of a sponge,
well then consider a little girls heart
to be that of a Bounty paper towel;
quick to pick up on when she's not wanted
and strong enough to absorb even the toughest spills.
Like when her self esteem gets thrown down a flight of
stairs.

It amazes me how confidence
can take years to build
and merely seconds
to tear down.
You should teach your daughter's how not to worship
mirrors,
but to appreciate their reflection.

Teach them that hide-n-seek
isn't just for the playground;
that it's
all too easy
to become consumed in another individual
to the point that you forget
who you are.
Teach your daughters that it's okay to feel lost
just as long as they don't lose themselves.

Teach them when they're young that
cuts and bruises
will never hurt as much as heartache
and there isn't a Barbie band-aid big enough
to protect her from love's battle wounds.
Teach your daughter's how to
stitch themselves back up;
Warn them
that broken hearts never completely heal,
but that it's crucial that they are held together.

They need to know that life
is full of loss;
a constant losing battle,
losing control, losing tempers,
losing patience, losing people
you love,
but the most precious thing lost
is not knowing how much you've gained.
Teach your daughters to hold it together;
to hold on.

CHRISTMAS IN JULY

This knot is unraveled
and I'm fully aware of how beautiful
my presence is.
So if you're gonna' tug on my heart strings,
tie them in a bow.
Then, gently place me
under the Christmas tree
for someone else
to open.
I'll be sure to leave the lights up
year round.

Russ Golata

Russ Golata is a Central Florida poet and organizer. He has been hosting 1st Monday's for the Orlando Poetry Group since 2006 at various locations.

His latest chapbook *Fragments of Chance* is available at Amazon.com

FLYING LESSONS

Has there ever been a moment
Where the dream of you meets my eyes
Entertaining my fingers in the folds of your skin
Wanting this embrace to last forever

You lying next to me with your perfect grin
Perplexing me into glassy ecstasies
The genuine velvet of your touch
Placing me into unknown worlds

The fascinations of your inner workings
Where our pierced moments collide
With the fireworks of my pounding heart
And the inescapable brightness of your charms

My ego swims in your pure energy
Flying into fullness of our love
Never wanting to land my feet
In the peace of our treasured bliss

TRANSLUCENT PERCEPTION

...within...
the velvet cover of darkness,
there is you...
alive in my dreams
...you...
one chance, one hope,
nobody but you,
...your light...
...your love...
~~emanates~~
fills my soul,
Shout it to the stars!
LOVE...LOVE...LOVE

UNCHAINED MELODY

Under the brilliant dark blue night sky,
The stars are all connected to the brain.
Silence broken by the whippoorwill's cry,
Blends music with excitement untamed.

Moon,gazing from his mountain of green cheese,
Casting a spell with mood altering light
Never, was a more perfect picture conceived
Nature the artist painting the world bright

Find a pathway from a heart to the stars
A connection to sights and sounds unseen
Float out like a constellation so far
To places that no one has ever been

Unfettered from the force of gravity
Love spreads through the world, finally set free...

Stephanie Salkin

Stephanie Salkin's poetry is published in *Tapestry*, a collection by the Tomoka chapter of the Florida State Poets Association. Her work also appears in children's literary and pet magazines. In addition to FSPA, Stephanie belongs to the Society of Children's Book Writers & Illustrators. She especially likes humor and wit.

RUNNING INTERFERENCE

You wanted to get him alone.
I'm sorry I got in the way.
I was getting ready to leave,
But, really, he asked me to stay.

I'm sorry I got in the way.
I know that you like him a lot.
But, really, he asked me to stay.
Yes, I realize he's totally hot.

I know that you like him a lot.
But maybe he just doesn't care.
Yes, I realize he's totally hot.
But, maybe—just maybe—you're not!

NOT EVEN A NIBBLE

It was a piscatory night.
I didn't know what to write
    So I was fishing.
I thought of you. It was a
     Fluke. I didn't mean to.
I wouldn't throw you a worm,
    Much less a thought,
Because you hooked me
And then you cast me off.

It was a piscatory day.
I didn't know what to say
    So I was fishing.
I talked to you. But it was
    Tripe. I didn't mean to.
I wouldn't throw you a line,
    Much less the slack,
Because you reeled me in and then
    You tossed me back.

It was a piscatory plight
    And I was sunk.

To Boy from Afar...

I love you,
Boy who sits three lunch tables away.
I don't know why.
It's something about your eyes,
Your mouth,
The way you swallow.
It doesn't much matter
Why.
I'd never dare talk to you,
Let alone touch you.
If only I could do something
Like save you from a tornado
That suddenly strikes these giant windows,
Shattering them into millions of shards,
The wind whipping them into missiles,
Spraying them across the cafeteria.
I sprint the treacherous distance to your table
And throw myself on you
To shield you.
My back becomes a lacework of glass.
The wind subsides.
You lean over me
And pluck out each bloody sliver,
One by one,
Tenderly.

Sean Crawford

Sean "Pix" Crawford is a poet originally from upstate New York. His style is diverse, ranging from addiction to love and relationships. He draws inspiration from friends, music, and everyday experience. Pix hopes to use his art to create awareness of social issues and the impact of words.

SUN OF LOVE

I hope one day to be reincarnated
Shine brighter than the past ones
No sun rays
Only love rays
Beaming down on you
To give you that affection you never received as a child
That kiss that won't cheat on you
That hug that won't walk out on you
That touch that won't hurt you
That voice that will never lie to you
I want to rise as much as I set
Give the world an equal balance
When I set
To rest for another day
The stars will watch over you
The moon will guide you
Because I would never leave you alone
I am that light in the moon
I am the reason it glows
So bright
Throughout the night
In the morning I shall rise again
As the moon and stars fill me in
On what happened
My day will begin
And I will shine brighter than suns before
But until then I will remain to walk amongst you
In human form

LOVE IS CRAZY

It's been almost 5 years.
And yea I may not cry tears
In front of you
But my heart still whimpers
And my body still shakes when I think of you.
I won't act like a punk or show much emotion
Because I am a man and you continued to tell me that men don't
do that
So I guess we are just supposed to keep it bottled up inside and
show sum pride
So of course these feelings I will hide
Like I'm am a gay man in the army
And I do not want to be exposed
Because it will block my goals
That I have worked so hard to get
I mean we have hurt each other like it was the new fad
And left each other too many times like we were one another's
dad
And we have went through so many apologies and "my bads"
But yet
I still love u
And when the words roll off my lips
My brain does, back flips
And my balance trips
Because it feels so weird to say
And then I think to myself
Am I okay
Is this normal for me to feel this way
Or am I just beginning to go crazy
And then I realize I'm just missing a piece of me
That became my best friend
That I want again
That used to be my lady
I'm telling you
Love is crazy

FOR YOU

All the sorrys in the world
Won't add up to how sorry I am
You have been so good to me
Never missed any of my poetry slams
Always telling me you could see me on Def Poetry Jam
Very supportive woman
And I was caring man
But had a funny way of showin it
Like when you messed up
Saying things like
"I knew you were gonna blow it"
The absent "pleases" and "thank yous"
When you did things you didn't have to
Even with no ring
You still try to do everything
I didn't accept you
I didn't respect you
I didn't want you
Played games with you
When someone could have really been loving you
Well I'm not going to waste anymore
Of your time
Cuz you're mine
I love you
And I'll do whatever I got to do
Because I want to be with only you

WolfSong (Steve Spellane)

I started writing at an early age as an outlet for my feelings, and to try and understand what was happening in my world, my life and in my thoughts. After a thirty year sabbatical I started writing again under the *nom de plume* of WolfSong. I offer them to you as a gift of the spirit of my muses. I hope you find them enjoyable and perhaps inspirational. After all, we poets do crave our immortality.

POET'S SONG

Snowy White Is The Paper Upon Which I Write;
Dark Is The Ink; As Black As The Night.
Together They Join, Words Form And Are One;
As One More Time; The Poet's Song is Sung.

The House Is Quiet Except For The Sounds
The Ghosts Always Make With One Person Around.
A Car Travels By, A Dog Barks In A Yard
I Can Hear My Heart Beating If I Listen Real Hard.

My Heart Now Flies, With A Lament And A Plea;
For A Thousand Miles It Cries As It Searches For Thee.
In Vain It Has Searched, And Remains Yet Alone;
Returns It Now; With A Howl . . . .That Chills To The Bone.

Heart Aches, Dawn Breaks As I Struggle To Rhyme;
The Cold Light Of Morning Through My Window Now Shines.
Birds Sing, Clocks Ring As I Pack Emptiness Away;
With A Well Rehearsed Smile; I Now Face The Day.

An Open Letter To A Friend

As a clear mountain lake reflects a deep blue sky, ... and
trees are painted with a pallet that only nature may provide.
So is your outer beauty a reflection of your inner radiance.
Enjoy the weekend; . . . This first true start to Autumn.
Walk daily among the trees . . . .until the cool winds force
them to shiver their last leaves to the ground.
Be sad at their apparent death and mourn the passing of the
warm times.
But know that this 'death" is only an illusion....And that
holds us not . . . . .or firm.
And that life , ...and love will bloom once again.
Be it in the deep snows of a winter's night,
With the first peeking of the crocus or the daffodil.
Or perhaps in the arms of a friend

Les Sirènes

Fluttering soft on angelic wings
The dark haired beauty in the heavens sings
Till brought to earth by arrows cruel flight
Lies she now twice pierced . . . .as day fades to night

Kindly sea brings end to pain
New sisters below the waves she gains
Strength returns where Poseidon dwells
Memory fades with the endless swells.

A vision of beauty rises from the sea
With a heartfelt song she call to me
Immune now to love's eternal stings
I travel now to where the siren sings

Alice Friedman

Alice R. Friedman's poetry appeared in *Poetry To Feed the Spirit*; *Connections*, A Collection of Poems by Poetry Ensemble of Orlando, and online at the Orlando Sentinel and WMFE-FM. She twice won first-prize for Non-Fiction in Mount Dora Writers Competitions. *What Now, Courage?* A book of poems was published in January 2012.

CLOSET ROMANCE

What's one to do when
a favorite blue jacket
slips an arm off its hanger
to embrace
the red lace blouse
beside it?

LEARNING JAZZERCISE®

One, two, pivot swivel
forward back reach.
Reach swivel
step out step *huh?*
    Kick ball change, ball change.
Right over left
left over right
chassè chassè.
Okay, okay
Hmmmm.

One, two pivot swivel
forward back
      darn
right over left
left over
      twist   down
    oops
think I'm bruised.

One, two pivot swivel
forward back reach.
Reach swivel
step out, step back
kick ball change, ball change
right over left
left over right
chassè chassè.
Okay, okay.
      Got it?
Maybe   not.

FIRST LOVE
BABYSITTING JENNY

Benjamin has fleas again
I feel them hopping under my bra
as we curl together
his purrs reduced to sighs
after a particularly tough cat fight.

I hear the crunch of tires
on the driveway.
Peter's home from fishing
a quick shower and he'll join Chloe for
Saturday night revelry
but first he
opens a can of Miller High Life
the Champagne of bottled beer
and we're in the back yard
he lets me take a sip as he
calls in some owls.
When he leaves Benjamin and I return
to our cuddle.

Amy Marie Aviles

A Milwaukee native, Amy M. Aviles was raised under the trop-
ical sun of the island of Puerto Rico. Immersed in a passionate
culture she developed a love for the arts in all its forms, poetry
being only one of them. Her creations cover a broad range of
venues from photographic compositions and painting to hu-
man skin kissed by the needle of her tattoo machine.

PAPER SKIN

I want to write me
as a poem of love
on your skin
with the tips
of my fingers.

Red is the color
of my ink,
red as the blood
that rushes through
my veins whispering
your name
as my heart beats.

On your skin,
my sin,
I will engrave all
my carnal desires,
with no shame,
and they melt
like butter.

And as I write
I can read me on you,
I can give me to you,
and you will have me
as I am.

CINNAMON

Your skin
smells like

CINNAMON.

Sweet,
nutty,
spicy,
and enticing.

Come
and season
my lips
my love.

You in my senses

I can hear you...
even a thousand miles away
when the wind brings
your voice to my ear.

I can see you...
even a thousand miles away
when I see the sun
shine in the horizon.

I can taste you...
even a thousand miles away
when the sweet morning dew
covers my lips.

I can speak to you...
even a thousand miles away
I just speak to you
out loud and I know you will hear me.

I have you...
even a thousand miles away
in all my senses
for ever and ever, Amen

Anton Kozel

Roaming through the world, I've landed in Orlando.
Art and counter-culture are bold aspects of my person-
ality. Writing has become more than self therapy to me;
it opened my eyes to the reality that psychology is a new
religion, and I'm inclined to the opposing side—how-
ever, with love most of all.

MIRAGE

The open fields of our intangible romance
are isolated, at the mercy of dreams.
I would give it all to be once again, but I'm not...
The blue sky will be in you, and in me
Upon my return

Living my absence from the alpha of your dreams
Absorbing the essence of your white hands
Entangled in the strands of my red hair
I would give it all to be once again, but I'm not...

Those consummated encounters,
have been engraved in the seas of our memory
So I will live in the cloister of your dreams, like a mirage
On my departure,
and the return.

Autumn Moon

Autumn moon, lonesome
Duet of peace and harmony
Luna, quiet and serene
Lighting barren valleys
And the rivers running through the fields

When in fall you contemplate
Nostalgic hearts,
You cover them with your white light,
Embraced in your silver heart

Nightly sonatas radiating fantasy
They are yours moon, oh moon of autumn
Your songs are beautiful whistles
In sound isolation, serenade of love and diamond poetry

SPENT

Those days (years!) I spent ever so carefree...

But, I looked at my passion then,
Murderus poeticus
and stabbed it in the gut; right where the butterflies revolt
Murderus poeticus
And, I killed it like a puppy I loved very much
Murderus poeticus

And, I saw it die and, I saw it fade
And, now I exhume every now and then the grave
in my own gut
I open it like you would a zippered bag and, let the dust
break free
And, the hair on my neck stands up,
because just like ghosts, beautiful memories come
to haunt me

Brian Vargecko

Brian Vargecko graduated from the University of Florida in 1993 with a degree in Theatre Performance. After many productions and a transition to writing, he published his first story, "I Know What's Good for You", in 2011. He intends on completing his MFA in Creative Writing and currently resides in Orlando with his wife and daughter.

ADVANCES

most beautiful sound ever heard –
immaculate singing hi the morning bird

most beautiful touch ever felt –
slippery sweep of the dolphin's pelt

most beautiful taste ever sipped –
sugary sweet finger-tip honey comb dipped

most beautiful fragrance ever sniffed –
mountain sky pilots copulating Heaven's lift

most beautiful sight ever seen –
melting snow, giant first glimpse of green

Passes like nature

VESPERTINE BEAUTY

When in Beauty with future's cast yet to be met,
  We must tangle our tears cry fortune's hate,
And strangle dear Desire with two mindless threats,
  And tell the whole world, you're not my mate,
Let's pray one day to be free to love,
  Unbound like God, like Him with graces weaving,
Creating all we will then speak of,
  With heads held high we'll put an end to grieving
Reward for the depths our friendship lies uprising,
  Darling how I love thee, and more with time,
Shall passion look to an unchartered arising,
  Let's sing our songs, let's shout our rhymes,
For the sweet bliss of Beauty has stirred life,
  And one precious day, I'll make you my wife.

THE ART OF OVERCOMING

Need sturdy trees perfectly placed I am done with my rake
Want life my to include a hammock
Well strung where I see all
I've got a map
Sextant and star
A bar nearby with a rough crowd I'm feared
I squint, scowl
Spit grab growl flip my coin with my thumb
Care not how much rum
Never get drunk
My hammock with mulch under it myself I chipped it
My Crusoe island, my Conrad ship
I launch my reed whip
Snap the mosquito dead I say Pow and pull another arrow
from my quiver, slay the boar
I do this for my family I work hard
Mow the yard
The sliding glass door I peer through saves lives of flies inside
lucky for now I'll get 'em
Inside, the kids romp past their mother setting the table
Damn she still looks good in a skirt, I'm lucky to have
married her so long ago
Wish I was Clint Eastwood sometimes
Wonder what she's cookin'?
Bet it smells better than this grass
But I love the smell of fresh cut grass who doesn't?
Don't want to know who doesn't
But if I had a hammock, boy, and time, trusty Nostromo
swings my machete, Friday at his heels he'll die alongside,
Stubb slices some whale we slice him, we wonder some need
to survive
I'm horny I think
Am I? This life won't let me It'll be dark soon
I could go for some shrimp
Been awhile

Whales Weep Not
Wonder if D.H. Lawrence ever considered a hammock
To any great length
Such as a hammock on a ship, a ship made from palms
Sailors erase old, write new psalms
Pack muskets, canons with alms
Surely D. H. Lawrence considered muskets, rest assured
I've got to put this tractor in the garage then wash up,
there's never any time
Rest? Rich! When?
As simple as Heaven is a hammock
Might accomplish something lying between palms
Learn French, oui
Love it these Florida leaves don't change, I'm tropical too,
native, tough
Knees don't bend like they used to though
You know, haven't been surfin', in awhile should see if I
still can
Tomorrow I'll take the kids they'll love it
Trade this yard for a beach
Buy me a hammock on the way back
Right after I buy me two trees
Sturdy palms that is

Carlton Johnson

Originally from Baltimore, Carlton has spent the past 5 years in Orlando. He is a teacher at The New Academy in Windermere. In his free time, he enjoys writing (or reading poetry), playing chess and travelling. He has recently returned to writing poetry after a long hiatus and enjoys the support of those at the Orlando First Monday group.

A Trip to the Science Center

Yesterday, you were excavating
with a small horse hair brush
the skull of a T. rex , fangs emerging
As large as your six year old hands
"Here", you exhorted, " get some safety glasses and a brush"
So we both moved the tan sand grains
Watching as jaw and eye socket and snout emerged
Splurging on the stillness of the moment
Between sands and hands and inquisitive glances,
The scientific alchemy and a child's wonder-filled revelry
While sifting through time and space.

RAINBOW

Burning tears streaking
Blue confusion and ocher desire
Yellow gratitude sits on the cold slate pallet
While Black hope bubbles up from underneath
A magma of forgotten dreams and passions
Tangerine melancholy is quickly covered over
with broad brushstrokes of vermilion
Serenity and copious amounts of turquoise vulnerability
flecked with pieces of mirror as it reflects
the light of the world
The true colors of the rainbow.

David Axelrod

Dr. David B. Axelrod, Suffolk County, Long Island's Poet Laureate from 2007-2009, is director of the Creative Happiness Institute in Daytona Beach, where he offers educational services to the public. He has published in hundreds of magazines and anthologies, as well as twenty books of poetry. He is the recipient of three Fulbright Awards including being the first official Fulbright Poet-in-Residence in the People's Republic of China.

ALL SALES ARE FINAL

There is no lemon law that covers lovers.
You shop around, go for a test drive.
You pay your money and take what
you get. Divorce is the junk yard.
If only we could return to confront
the dealer, "The rear end is noisy
and the transmission leaks." No
way to get your money back
when you fall in love. But what
a ride, tearing out of that parking
lot with a giddy smile, that shine
that says everything is new—even
that new smell, which most agree
is carcinogenic, but who cares?
That's what you are buying—
new roads to travel. Only, when
the parts fail, there is no turning back,
no bumper to bumper warranty—just
the wrecker, someone you give
your title, and one last look
for small change under the seat.

Is It Love?

Is it love we want on a rainy
night, wishing the patter
were something more than
gutters and gusts; touching,
not tires sluicing through
wet streets? Or do we want
just sunrise to rescue us
so we can raise the cover,
stretch, right foot down,
then left to do what we must
by habit? Perhaps that's all
we wish for at this point—
to live on our own, not needing
whom to comfort us like some scared
kid crying in the dark or shrinking
with each thunder clap. Better,
be careful what you wish.
Because the sun can't shine
all the time we have the night—
soothing its dark way into creases,
lubricating dreams, offering
what us its darker reality.

AFTER I CAUGHT MY GIRLFRIEND

After I caught my girlfriend
in bed with another man—
worse, a fellow writer whose
talent made me jealous—
I took to my car and drove
two hundred miles in no
direction. The engine did
not overheat or fume. Only
I emitted odorous epitaphs
and curses no catalytic
converter could captured.
Jilted lovers learn to burn
their sorrows into raptures.

Hope Esprit

Each of us is living out our own book of poetry. "I Wear Him Well And other poems about love and life," "Breathing Flowers" and "Kitchen Kisses" (self-published e-books on Amazon), chronicle mine. Lifelong writer/poet/traveler from upstate NY. New to Central Florida. At home, anywhere, with my poetry.

THE PUDDLE

Tears.
They will flow.
Each one,
a symbol.
A feeling.
A manifestation.
My face,
then
wiped away.
Each drop.
Each wipe.
A lessening...
The pain...
Perhaps.
Some day,
the tears
will be dry...
So, too
will be
the puddle
of pain,
currently
my heart.
Still beating.
Still longing.
For you...

LOVABLE ME

I don't know what to expect from you.
I only know what my mom thought true.
The crux hides inside, in mystery.
Open eyes, quite possible to see.
She said:
The song in your heart,
The shine in your eyes,
The sounds in your voice,
The care in your sighs.
I am lovable
Beneath my beauty.
Beautiful baby,
Lovable Me.

Teachers know I was always quite shy.
Enlightened spirit, afraid: Ask Why!
Mind home on Mom, alone without me.
Only takes one--an interest, you see.
She said:
The words from your lips,
The strength of your tone,
The stare in your cheeks,
The heart left at home.
I am lovable
Beneath my beauty.
Beautiful child,
Lovable Me.

The boys have always flocked around me.
Unwilling to give; want it for free.
Preconceived views: Be Her, Can You Please?
Insecure--Let Me Be Me, With Ease!
She said:
The blue in your eyes,
The sharp in your mind,

The song in your soul,
The One, you will find.
I am lovable
Beneath my beauty.
Beautiful person,
Lovable Me.

Here I am, complex and grown up, see.
Unapologetic: I Am Me!
Beauty is wasted, left inside thee.
Treat me right, world; shower love on me!
She said:
The sun on your teeth,
The gifts that you give,
The love in your loins,
The heart that you live.
I am lovable
Beneath my beauty.
Beautiful woman,
Lovable Me.

HEART ARRIVED

Issue yourself a passport.
Visit the country of Fall Apart.
Learn the language of pain and sorrow,
Frequent flyers, now prisoners, your heart.

Break down, while there, hang it out.
New cuisine, tour of tears, they will come.
Sometimes strong (sights) resemble the weak.
Locked heart, too much rum, makes you numb...

Beg, bars of bitterness, be gone!
Sun seen, from the plane window, second soul.
Impostor through customs, afraid no more.
Heart arrived, welcoming visitors, whole.

Elaine Person

Elaine Person performs original poetry and stories, writes scripts, lyrics, "person"alized poems and stories, and teaches workshops. Her parody "King Arthur" was in Random House's "A Century of College Humor." Elaine's stories, "I'm A Person" and "Glossed Over," appeared in Florida Writers Association anthologies. Email her at Lnprsn@aol.com.

ODE TO A RED LIGHT

I love a red traffic light
Then I can put my makeup on right
But if it's dark
I'll look a fright.
Trying to put it on at night.

Red light, time giver to me
I wake up in the morning, then I flee
I would look badly
If it weren't for thee.
Red light you are all I see.

I get time to comb my hair
Floss my teeth
Phone my friend Claire
Put on my shoes
Shave my legs
Read the paper
Eat some eggs
Drink some coffee
Finish getting dressed
Write a poem
Have a quick rest.

Now it's green and I must go
Until next time I'll miss you so.

You Woke Me Up

You woke me up–not like my mother in the morning
but like Cary Grant kissing Eva-Marie Saint on the train and
on the neck.
Like a bear coming out of hibernation–starving, ravenous to
take in something new.
You woke me up–grabbed my eyelids and rolled them open
like old-fashioned window shades,
forced me to look at you, laser-like.
You woke me up–like hot, brown, steamy liquid, scent
wafting and welcoming from behind the kitchen door.
Not like a clock radio screaming sales into my ears.
You woke me up from verbal slumber, aching hunger,
encumbered with boredom, anger, and analysis.
You woke me up, yanked me up from the dark pit into
Technicolor swirls, dancing toe-point, swaying, (flying,)
floating like runaway leaves in autumn.
You woke me up from fake dreams to real ones, nightmares
to utopia.
My stifled smiles letting loose like a Champagne bottle on
New Year's Eve.
And you woke me up from the can'ts and chants of "No,"
the shouldn'ts and couldn'ts of woe.
Why not? I like being awakened by you.
You woke me up.

IT COULD HAPPEN TO YOU

Beware the Man
Who gives flowers too soon.
His love will wilt
Before the flowers bloom.

Frank Defulgenti

Frank DeF is raised in and around Philly and South Jersey. His background in psychology and automotive technology reflect his writing style which he refers to as "soul searching with an edge." He has five books published: "Here We Reach The Beginning," "Death is in my Coffee," "Deeper Now," "The Erotic Poetry of Frank DeF," and "Flux."

GASOLINE

you are what it means
to last forever

invested interest
organic liquid
the you in myself
what
matters most
if nothing else

your kiss
is octane 94
you are more
true
than you know

Gene Murphy

Gene Murphy, a native of Brooklyn, N.Y., and a graduate of New York University, was a newspaper and magazine reporter and editor in New Jersey, and manager of communications for a major gas and electricity utility in that state, before retiring and settling in Palm Coast, Florida in 2000.

UNTITLED, UNTITLED

When is it Spring, and the heart not a dancer,
eyes slow in shaking the waned-winter's cold
time but a space, left for remembering?
When one is old, when one is old.

Where is the glance, ever desperate, so lost
eyes full of gamble that never have won
steeled for the shock the hour-glass holds?
With the forlorn one, the forlorn one.

But, ah, there's the smile, fresh as new clover,
eyes touching gently as a new velvet glove
Stock still, O time, for this, the enchanted:
The young love, the young love.

THE HOLE IN THE FENCE

It was an aluminum canoe, 16 feet long
I ran it in whitewater only once
On it, a poor paddler can go wrong
and wind up a wet and angry dunce.

 I'd struggle to get it atop the car, then lash it down
and motor north from Jersey, to Seven Lakes Drive,
a road that winds past lakes like diamonds in a crown
that sparkle in the morning sun; one felt glad to be alive.

We'd choose Sebago, the wife and I, to paddle
I aft, Patricia forward, but she would, mostly, rest.
It's tranquil to drift across a giant puddle
and in fourth stage lymphoma, tranquility is best.

I glued a plastic name on the bow of the canoe
It read "Patsy's Panacea" and it was, indeed
she smiled; it was in her favorite color, blue
she ran her fingers across it, as if they, too, could read.

Mountain laurel bloomed along Sebago's shore
but for the next few years only rain, only snow
touched Patsy's Panacea -- the laurel she did adore
bloomed on unseen, as we watched lymphoma grow.

 It grew, then ceased, but only in one way does lymphoma
cease
It claimed this wistful, tranquil lady of the lakes in 1991
Patsy's Panacea then sat in a fenced yard, lacquered with
grease,
its days of floating in a tranquil pond to ease her pain were
done.

Then someone fancied the craft and on a moonless summer
night,
cut a perfect circle out of the fence, and spirited my boat
away
it seemed so apt; some spirit, I believe, on a bitter winter
night
cut a circle in the fabric of my life, and spirited Patricia
straightaway.

I like to think that somewhere, on a tranquil lake, she now
can drift
in early spring, with mountain laurel, everbearing, at her
fingertip.
As for the thoughtless thief, I hope fate gives him short,
short shrift,
and in an angry river, while waters roar, may my treasured
vessel flip.

HAPPY BIRTHDAY — IT WAS TODAY?

I leaned one day too far, looking down a well
and a treasured lighter slid from a shirt pocket
I watched it glittering its way down the depths
and in the innocence romantics seem to have
delicately raised the well's bucket, bit by bit
but it held only water, and an empty wish.
I ceased to worry, years ago, and,
patting empty pockets where cash should have been
I shrug. I would have only spent it, needlessly.
But some things I have lost have hurt so
that there is no recovery from the blow.
I lost a loved one of great beauty and for years
blamed God for such a senseless act.
But God had let me find her, I decided,
and gave us years that were a priceless gift
and, like the loving God he is, in time,
brought to my life one who, with patient care
puts up with soiled socks dropped everywhere,
reading matter of all kinds in every corner.
She has this simple flaw that I can live with;
she's found a loser who she thinks has value
And God has let this loser share her life,
her mornings, noons, and nights and on this day,
her birthday.
Now where did I put her gift?

Gillian Wolfe

Gillian was born in London, England and immigrated at a young age to Canada, where her four children still reside. She now lives in Florida with her husband, Joe, and their two dogs, one cat and a goldfish. She enjoys writing, painting, volunteering, and spending time with family and friends.

PLEASE

Please, don't check out early
the best is yet to come.
There is hope around the corner
with love and joy and song.
Look up and see the wonder
past the clouds of tears and pain
for the light is still there shining
a life that bears your name.

Please, don't check out early
the best is yet to come.
Choose to fight and stand up
to people filled with hate,
Don't let them give you reason
to end your beauty and your fame
for there's a future waiting for you
that belies their hurtful names.

Please, don't check out early
your best is yet to come,
We need your contribution
to the symphony of life.
Without your living spirit
we all suffer in the loss,
Reach out your hand and take mine-
for our best is yet to come.

WE ARE FAMILY

You are my family;
many and varied,
unique and tied
together with
a cord of love.

We work together
to encourage the sick,
feed the poor
and bring hope
to the lonely.

Yet, still I am called
a foreigner,
A label that suggests
separation, exclusion
and distance.

A foreigner because
of my birth place?
the colour of my skin?
my sexual orientation?
All gifts from my Creator.

There is no foreigner
to the Source of Life.
No one is
unwanted, unacceptable,
or ever excluded.
We are family
no matter what
you may do or say,
or believe to be true.
We are all God's family.

Sitting on a Bench

Sitting on a bench
quiet and peaceful
with chatter and music
all around me.
A water fountain
dances skyward
playing with the angels
who cast a blanket
of lacy grace over all
who stop and listen.
There are not many
who stop, most are busy
rushing to and fro
afraid to miss something
"important".
When in reality they miss
the smile of God,
the peace of knowing
all is well
for love is all around.

Joe Wolfe

Born and raised in the province of Saskatchewan, Canada, Joe now makes his home with his wife Gillian in Florida. His poetic works came as a creative outlet while going to university, and courting. Today his creativity is used mainly for software development.

GROWING

Two seeds lay on the ground.
Within their hull lay the instinct for growth.
Upon them sat a heavy stone.
Roots dove for nourishment, stems reached for light.
The stone did not yield and yet the stems grew.
Sickly white, twisted, unsure but still reaching for Life.

Finding the sun's loving caress,
the plants retreat to the dark safety of the known.
But having been touched once by Life,
the retreat cannot last.
Their heads once more peep around the stone,
and breath fresh air.

Growth giving sap must travel,
through the twisted, knarled, painful path
that marks each plant's journey.
As it does the plants stretch,
towards Life, each other, and others.
Soon all can see the plants' triumph.

Working together the plants accomplish what
could not be done while to solitude they kept.
The stone's thrown off, they expose their weakness.
Life's light turns the weakness to strength.
The burden cast aside,
two trees grow entwined.

The winds of evil do their worst,
but each tree supports the other,
and each trial strengthens their trunks.
There is a lesson in a mustard seed's faith.
The smallest seed when nurtured by Love,
becomes a tree where little birds choose to make their nest.

I AM FILLED

I am filled, my cup overflowing,
Yet someone keeps pouring the wine of love.
No longer do I need to wait for scraps from the table,
like a begging dog,
For she has invited me to join the feast.
I feel inadequate to return the favor.
For too long the loving nature has been fettered,
Now allowed to be free the immobilized wings ache,
There is too much ground to be covered,
and too little power.
Please, don't leave me if I fail you.
In time the exercise of love
Will strengthen the atrophied wings.
Then will I be able to hunt,
To provide game for the feast.
For now, I hope that my small offerings
Will be seen as my best effort to please,
The one who has filled me with love to overflowing.

Kristen DeFlorio

I create thoughts to escape the bondage of a broken mind, releasing the energy from a glued together heart. The feeling to evoke my emotions through writing, makes me feel whole again. I love to paint with my words to try to create a visual for a particular moment.

THE MISPLACED NOTE

Here sitting, the warmth of the cabin is inviting
While the blizzard beats on the window panes

Dipping the feather in the ink: I start to write feverishly

To my sweetest daffodil:
Do you remember the moss, where we sat under the stars?
Pointing out saturn and counting out the rings?

I cover with a blanket, shivering a tad
Putting more wood into the flames
I crumble the paper: I begin again
To my delicate sunflower:
I have tried and tried with no avail
To put words down to express my heart

Sipping my tea, trying to stay awake
Lighting the candles nearest to me
I gently weep: trying to illustrate my love for thee

To my yellow violet:
When I needed affection and comfort
You were there, during my darkest hour

Looking over to a pile: I sigh
It had been ages since hearing from Marigold
I placed the failed attempts into the fire

To my lovely dandelion:
Wishing you knew how much I care for you
But you will never receive these letters
The Willow Tree

Painting the sunset: moved beyond the beauty
The crickets play a song: just for me
A perfect symphony of joyous harmony

Sitting here: remembering the days
Where we pushed through the meadows
And collapsed: to relax

Standing under the canopy of tranquility
You grab my hand, saying: marry me
My face lighting up like fireworks: smiling

Wishing my daydream would come true
The moon starts to push through
Leaning against the tree: the wind sang, would you?

THE GATEKEEPER

He stood at the turning point: floating effortlessly
And I approached slowly: timidly touching the stepping stones
The lake was clear: glowing green effervesces

He held a lamp: filled with molten sap
And I peered closer: a faceless entity
The boat was coming nearly: creaking slowly

Get in and your head will be cleared, he announced
And I carefully approached: fearful of touching the water
The vessel advanced to the dock: no captain could be seen

Do you see this beacon?
It holds your life: right at my fingertips
And you have two choices, he simply stated

What are they?
There must be a price to pay for this sort of knowledge
I have decisions to be made, I replied cautiously

Two shingles will be had when you arrive here again
The first: to have loved intensely but with a rocky journey
The second: to love mildly with effort and ease
A ruling must be made, he retorted

 You must be death then, your cloaked figure is familiar
What a prospect, what a feeling, what a choice
If I pick the latter: I will not have tasted yearning
If I select the primary: I will have experienced true ardor

Your time is almost up or you will stay here
Have you made up your mind?
You must select now! .... he commanded

I claim passion! tenderness! enchantment!

And the somber immortal accepted the pact.

THE WILLOW TREE

Painting the sunset: moved beyond the beauty
The crickets play a song: just for me
A perfect symphony of joyous harmony

 Sitting here: remembering the days
Where we pushed through the meadows
And collapsed: to relax

 Standing under the canopy of tranquility
You grab my hand, saying: marry me
My face lighting up like fireworks: smiling

Wishing my daydream would come true
The moon starts to push through
Leaning against the tree: the wind sang, would you?

Kristine Torgerson

My poetry is raw, unadulterated and unfiltered, through formal training. Experience has been my teacher and facing truth, my discipline. A soul's uncovering of wounds with words and also its therapeutic balm. In sharing, my desire is to touch others who are brave enough and wish to unsheathe their souls and "stand naked in the rain"

RASHOMON

I hold you in a tear
sitting on my lash
afraid to blink
To loss you to a box of Kleenex
I played a harp song
strung by the laughter of fresh love
A path now laid in sounds of sorrow
whispered in the ears of angels
Like the mountains of Himalaya
our time frozen
A silent snow
Moonlight of our nights
reflected in a of glass of wine
Toast to lovemaking memories
A nightingale's throbbing throat
echoes the passion laden sheets
Now songbird stands on withered branch
My soul casts a shadow against the wall
The harp song has been sung
A Burmese ruby
A jewel
returned to the earth
A buried heart
I see the story thru a single eye

SIGHS

The setting sun cusps the distant horizon
in the day's parting embrace
It's raining so softly
the pitter patter soon a memory
As the pale moon sits on the lip of the lake
Waiting
An invited guest on a door stoop, to be asked in
Night not having entered its' full glory
The earth holds its breath
As the frog choruses serenade swamp lovers
Raises a courting ruckus
Then the night shadows come out
to play a cat and mouse game with imaginations
Lightening bugs on patrol flicker warnings
An evening breeze skips across my skin
Bringing visions
A desert oasis or a mirage
Smells of dates and figs cascades my senses
I hear the tinkling of ice in frosted glass
Feeling the cool hand of my lover
slip under my blouse
and rest as a feathers' breath
on the small of my back
Then kissing deeply the pooled essence
of mint julep lips
All on a summer's night.

CAUGHT IN THE CHECKOUT

He offers you a cavernous smile
You fall into it like sky diving
Waiting for the chute to open
The pop/ the jerk
Back to reality
You better watch where you're going
You'll need a headlamp for this one
He's the one who could make you
act like a cartoon character
running off a cliff
Beep, beep
Watch out you're falling
Before you know it
This time no parachute
You could end up a green Gumby
Splat on the ground
Are there any shovels around
to clean up the mess?
Why'd you have to catch his eye?
Why'd he have to smile that smile?
The stars are suppose to stay in the sky
Where's the warning sign?
"No star gazing in the checkout line"
You'd have been safer with your nose
in the gossip rags
Brad and Angelina
they only have eyes for each other
To late the Hagen Daz
is melting to fantasized thoughts
Newest flavor "Damp, Wet 'en Wild"
Each spoonful a playful nibble on that
right ear, the one with the freckle
and blond semi curl you'll have to
push out of the way with your tongue

OOPs
Damn these checkout lines
always move too fast!
Beep, beep

Laurie Borrego

Laurie Borrego lives in a quiet rural area of Florida. Even with the onset of a steady stream of traffic on our main roads, the loll driving the last ten miles to home brings a sense of disconnect of time rushing to catch up, inviting the senses to grasp the importance of everyday occurrences. Writers live in their heads at places yet unseen, packing lightly to travel the experience.

Fin

He told me
saying "I love you" was stupid.
Somewhere between the sheets
lies his disregarded emperor's clothes.
I knew his albatross by name.
At twilight I watched a mass of dragonflies
buzz sinuously feasting
on the bounty of the summer rain.
My hand opened the car door.
I prepared myself
for the washboard dirt roads
I had to drive.
He had turned
left
in the house before I stepped outside.
I drove a very long way before thinking
"Will I ever see so many dragonflies in one place again?"

I HAVE A TREASURE CHEST ...

a seven by five inch box
made from a mahogany tree
by an unknown Haitian.
A carver's story of dirt roads
he walks lined with thatched roof houses
and sago palms.

Every time I open it,
the beauty of it
makes my hands tremble
and stops my heart.

Inside, one piece of paper
of a butterfly
with rainbow wings.

"Oh, grandma!", my grandson said,
"You have a treasure chest. What is in it?"
I took the box off the buffet
showing him detailed panorama etchings.
Again he asked me what was inside.
I opened the exquisitely carved lid,
"See, it is empty."

I set the box back on the buffet,
"We leave it here to look at it."

He pulled his handmade butterfly out of his
pants pocket closing the box lid again.

I have a treasure chest.

WANTING TO FIND TIBET

I ventured for 45 minutes in traffic
past stop lights, cars in decisive thought, "left, no right",
busy policeman discreetly placating their next paycheck,
doe eyed pedestrians risking limbs to cross streets quick as
rabbits,
some poke tortoise fashion facilitating vulture ambulance
chasers.

Parallel parking on the street a block from the Dandelion
Cafe,
where I assured myself mysteries of millennium ceased
to bewilder and were disheveled.
I sat patient, a feigned composure, inside my gut
a squirrel darted furiously across lost habitat
searching for acorns to foil a sparse feast in winter.

After seductive secret thumb twiddles,
a parade of unencumbered monks arrived.

Our promised venue to enlightenment.
The email read:
Today Only! Our Friends at the Dandelion Cafe
invite you to celebrate a Chorus of Blessings by
Tibet's Drepung Loseling Monastery Monks.

Messiah in heaven flinched,
the monks in red robes smiling calm.
One standing next to me,
his eyes imploring me to question
"What is real, gracious one?"

He answered, "What you think is real."
the same calm moved swift to his eyes.

I thought peace must be somewhere
in there and determined to find it,
I said, "My friend, Harley, does not think what I tell him is
real."
"Harley does not see what you see," the monk as perplexed
as I was
waited for someone to cue his next move.

Of course, my mother would have asked if I was lying.

Mary McBride

At one time I expected to be a published author but eventually found my voice in art. However, words still stir and blend into songs from my heart on occasion. I've written fiction and poetry since elementary school and eventually graduated from Stetson University when I was 51 with a major in art and minors in English, women's studies and art history.

THE BEAR WENT OVER THE MOUNTAIN

He crashed through the brush
lowly growls more a conversation with himself
than a warning of his coming

I could smell his rancid fur before he appeared
his humid fish breath enveloped the clearing
making it hard to breathe

When he dropped his heavy head onto my shoulder
drool dripping on my breast
I felt old scars of claw marks on my back itch

He rubbed his muzzle on my neck
and I mumbled go away Old Bear
don't stir old memories

He stumbled away through the forest
never sure why he was rejected
not understanding his transgressions

He staggered with halting gait
over the mountain into the sunset
bemused grin in place

THE GARDEN GATE IS OPEN

The bear came into my yard
and I fed him grilled salmon,
fresh baked bread,
and blueberry muffins.
He swayed back and forth
rumbling his appreciation,
and stayed to tell me forest stories,
while cleaning his whiskers.
Once I reached out,
but he ran into the woods.
Now he lumbers back and forth,
outside my gate, sniffing the air.
        Today, I bought tuna steaks.

Mary-Ann Westbrook

Mary-Ann was born and raised in Syracuse, NY. She and her husband Jon lived in the Catskill Mountains for a time, then raised a family in Buffalo, NY. Upon retiring they traveled full-time in a recreational vehicle for several years before settling in Ormond Beach. She won first place in the Atlantic Center for the Arts Poetry Slam in 2006 and is currently president of the Tomoka Poets.

DAISY POWER

He loves me, he loves me not
    the daisy holds the key
Pansies merely smile and nod
    never saying what's to be

Daffodils will sing of Spring
    but love they do not see
So they'll not tell me if he does
    not even for a fee

Roses are supposed to say it
    but this I do decree
Their velvet beauty though unsurpassed
    is silent in my reverie

Violets of purple hue
    spread out across the lea
So tiny, sweet and knowing
    can they see him on bended knee?

No, I must wait for the daisy's sign
    and hope it speaks to me
He loves me, he loves me not
    I'll have to wait and see

LATE NIGHT CALL

rriinngg

Hello my love
I missed you today
it's lonely here
since you went away.

    You too? I knew

 I took a walk
and saw you there
reached that spot
you were nowhere

    You too? I knew

I miss your touch
so gently felt
That soft caress?
it makes me melt.

    You too? I knew

 I taste your kiss
when I'm asleep
your lips so soft
my heart could weep

    You too? I knew

Good-by my love
I know it's late
but tomorrow?
I can not wait

    You too? I knew!

THE WEDDING

Today is the day
you pledge with your heart
to love one another
till death do you part

From this day forward
your love will grow
to a comfort and contentment
that only you can know

The bond that you form
will make you strong
to ease those times
when things seem to go wrong

Your friends are all here
to witness this day
They give you best wishes
as we send you on your way

For love from your family
you need never ask
We all give you our blessing
and assign only this task

 As time moves on
through days and years
depend on each other
and have no fears

Remember this day
when you pledged with your heart
to love one another
till death do you part

Mila Golata

Born a New Yorker, I have lived in Florida for over twenty years. Meeting my husband's poetry family has exposed me to many creative and talented artists. The emotions and passions they arouse with their words always impresses me. A closet poet, I am baby stepping towards opening the door.

TENDER TOUCHES

Tender touches
I touch your skin
Fingers floating
My fingers trace
Gliding over
I lose myself
Makes me feel
My head floats
Waves of pleasure
Creating visions
Breath comes slowly
Growing fast
Gazing deep
Feels like drowning
Explosive energy
Uniting our souls
Tender touches
All around

inviting and warm
with hair so soft
ever calm
your fingers form
silky skin
to senses within
 as if aloft
in clouds of thoughts
sounds of sighs
in my mind
half alive
ecstatic high
in truest eyes
in bluest skies
fills the air
to ONE universal soul
everywhere
for us to share.

LOVE

You speak to me of love
And to show you love
But how to show
Something so personal
Without
Touching
Kissing
Hugging
It is not possible
To show love
With mere words
Love
Isn't taught,
Per se
It is felt
It is shared
It is shown
Love
A marvel
So simple
So profound
Love
A miraculous
Blessing,
Finding
A soulmate
Love
Sweet
Delicious
Profoundly sensual
Love
A fleeting fantasy
To enjoy
Without expectancies
Without regrets
Without restrictions
Love
Unconditional exchange
International language
Eternal desire

Nena Larieze Weinsteiger

Why I write ... I began writing when I was eleven years old. My mother had come home from the hospital after a brief remission, and was given three days to live. My writing began as prayers that morphed into poetry, which progressed to fiction and nonfiction. I lost my mother, but I have never lost my passion to write.

ECONOMIC ESCAPE

When the days are long, I long for you.

When times are tough, I crave your touch,
for you to cover me up with our silk comforter,

for you to rebuild the sand castle of my motivation,
when it is crumbling,

for you to whisper *sweet somethings*
into my aching ear.

After a ten hour shift, we often forget the worth of love
of moments that repeat as silent movies in our minds—

bursts of uncontrollable laughter,
flashes of clandestine smiles.

When the world crumbles, you hold me upright,
enclose me within your arms and

wrap me within the walls of our home—
where we can shut out the whole world.

DARE SHARE

I promise not to allow the strokes of my past the privilege
to paint our future.

I promise to accept you, for who you are,
whether your hair is untamed,
like the student's of Berkeley, or
short like the insurance agents we are.

I will not wed my heart to you, without first a ceremony of
truth.

I promise to appreciate your subtle acts of kindness, and to
never take for granted the way your eyes, like Flagstaff
mocha,
swirl, in awe of my presence.

I promise to speak in obsolete vernaculars—
a language all our own, with "No way, Juan Jose's" and
"Geez, Lariezes",
just because we can.

I promise to fight your battles with the same conviction that
I fight my own.
Art and activism is our scripture, and
The Grand Canyon, our place of worship.

With this, I also promise to leave you, if I am suffering;
I promise not to be a martyr of what cannot be.

I promise to allow life to shelter us.
I take your hand and together we
throw pebbles into the Canyon, like wishes
we don't dare share.

WE BEGAN

We began as a hand on a shoulder, then
fingers intertwined. We began as

a first kiss, in the
freezing cold of early February,

and there awoke a love, far removed
from the consumerism of Valentine's Day.

We began as friends, and
now our toes cramp in
synchronicity.

We began as many great loves do—
unaware,
unsure, and
uninhibited.

Peter Gordon

After a 30 year career in television and theatre, Peter is happy to be a full time writer. He's written for local Orlando publications, national newspapers, and national baseball magazines. He holds degrees from Yale and CMU. Peter and his wife Ellen live in Orlando with their three boys.

THE WAY IT SHOULD HAVE HAPPENED

Count all our change.
Do we have enough for beer?
Those last two soldiers look lonely
Behind some buzzing fluorescents
Guarding the deep recesses of
Sal's Convenience Store fridge.

We'll skip across Sheep Meadow
Where oak trees obscure the skyline
Bees buzz like the old days
When the Canarsie Indians sought honey
To flavor savory smoke
And sweeten their long houses

Beer buzz fuzzes our brains
Stumbling over obscure sidewalk cracks
We hang on each other
All the way back to your flat
Kicking off loafers
We tumble together

Lie in pools of sweat
Bare breeze ruffles the white blinds
Listen to the street buzz
Outside your window
Crowds dancing like bees dance
Savoring mysterious sweet pleasures

NIGHT GAME

Crouch in the batter's box. Dig toes in the dirt.
Peer over my left shoulder toward the mound
Hands back and high.
Keep my eye on the poems flung at me.

Fat juicy words float up to the plate
Then dart towards my knees
Nouns and verbs whiz by
To thump against the backstop.

I swing at everything.

Sometimes I whiff wildly
Spinning around in the dirt
Sometimes barely tip one
That squibs foul down the baseline.

When I connect
Words line back up the middle
Or down the line in left
Rolling toward the fence as I slide into second

And sometimes a sweet shiver runs
From the tip of my pen to my shoulders
Words soar high and far
Against the night sky

Falling over the fence
To land in verses straight and true
I circle the bases
Home.

LAVENDER

You wore that scent
Like a skintight dress
I smell it on your picture and
The worn wooden frame

It lingers in odd attic corners
Bureau drawers
Floating over yellow and blue
Sun dresses hung neatly in the closet

I inhale
You're all around me
Deep within my lungs
Tangled in my legs

And I forget
The ghost dance
The barren bed
The heavy stone with your name
The small rocks piled on top

Robert Gibbons

Robert Gibbons is originally from Belle Glade, Florida. He is the oldest of five children from a Palm Beach County elementary school teacher of more than thirty years. A graduate Florida A&M University, Robert has taught in several school districts and now works as an English Specialist for the Renaissance Charter High School of Innovation of East Harlem (Manhattan), New York City.

SIT IN MY MOUTH

 a certain time of year
my grandmother will give us
castor and cod liver oils
and honestly I can't remember
ever having any medical issues
besides the usual broken bones
that boys sometimes have
the closeness I have
is a hair line
fractures of my elbow
a stump- toe tree
in the eighth grade
is just a hairline
a thin line
between aloe and castoria
the boil of grandma's pot
only those natural remedies
that grandmothers know
she will never tell
I never ask

I MADE A SLOW START

I graze like a blue heron
from the marching band fields
of Belle Glade the raiding
of the muck leading me
to the highest of seven hills
in Tallahassee I have seen
those hills before on my summer
trips to southern Georgia
we were not accustomed
to red clay of my great-grandmother's
only the variety only the muck
of the everglades
on the cane trucks only the smell
of a burning sugar cane in October
only the sweat
beading down her back
after she returns
from the clothes line
how can you tell me not
to worship the ancestors
that grandmother is not a metaphor
she went to the line
and never came back
this is my sign

I HAVE LONG WONDERED WHAT MY STRENGTHS WERE AS A WRITER
(*for: Theodore Roethke*)

If I am to obtain craft
I must go back
to the mud pies
of a fresh Florida rain
to my grandma's house
on tenth street
to run across the field
the house is closed
after the funeral
and now all that's left
is memory and pity
I did not record it
maybe as Roethke says
I am just a mere reporter
and not an astronomer
my reach is there
a creative worker
during these times
I went to the cornfield
will organize my ears
in rows as my grandmother
watches over my shoulder
this is only important to me
should the entire world
know I am migrant hands
all I know is field work
the sweat of one-thousand suns
responsible forthe blackening
of my boots the soot
of the sugar mill the browning
of the grain and now
I can't forget I sit
idle too long
in her beige Buick

Ryan Hayes

Ryan Hayes is a 29-year-old teacher/coach/poet. He teaches middle and high school aged students with learning and behavioral disabilities. He draws inspiration from his parents.

POEM #1

Upon a road of desolute
A struggling man with fractured hands
Contemplates whether the truth
Was ever real or just imagined lands,
Devised by those whose powers to be
Are stronger than the worlds combined
They say hard work and love will set you free,
But is this reciprocated by the other side
What do they know about real life
Vacations, yachts and fast cars and gold,
The allure of such only brings strife
But the men up high still claim to know,
For the people or for the few
Their stench and odor is in the air,
While my people's hearts shine through
The chosen ones do not play fair,
Suppressed by life and how it's played
A struggling man with fractured hands
Contemplates an early grave
It would be easy as they'd understand,
However something deep keeps him alive
As an honest man has help from inside,
He hears a voice from within
Urging him to try again
And so the man with fractured hands,
Rises for a second chance
To show the ones that sit up high
That an honest man will always survive,
Through thick and thin, blood, sweat and tears
We will remain forever years.

DREAMS

In denial of things gone wrong,
Life has become a tragic song
Thinking back on yesterday,
Worry free and joyful play,
Love surrounded every room
Family was beauty, like a rose in bloom
As we grow, situations arise
Events can bring an awful demise
How am I supposed to cope,
It's as if I've lost my only hope,
What once was real has morphed to clear
The only feeling left is fear,
What should a lion do when scared,
He cannot show it for then he is bare,
A fighter must regain his form
And ready himself for the storm,
Dreams inside must stay alive
This is the only way to survive.

Sandra Beaulieu

A writer and published author of poetry, Florida tales and children's books, Sandy moved here from Massachusetts with her family in 1970 and has been writing poetry since High School. Other creative endeavors include storyteller, ventriloquist, and artist.

NEW LOVE

 Did I find you or you find me
How did we come to be
Or was it just fate
That first date
You brought new life back into my weary soul
So kind and gentle thoughtful too
Considerate never demanding
The way you look into my eyes
And hold my hand
Your touch sends shivers up and down my spine

ANGER

What is anger
    red or blue
Am I mad
    at me or you
Is it sadness
    blame or fear
To almost lose
    someone so dear
What is anger
    fists or tears
Is there no one
    there who hears
Hears me crying
    in the night
Come and hold me
    hold me tight
Wrap your arms
    around me please
All this anger
    you can ease
What is anger
    friend or foe
How can I change
    to high from low
A friend who's there
    to really care
That's all I need
    my self to feed
And make me whole
    and heal my soul

LAURIE

I didn't know her very long
Her stay here was all too brief
She gave my heart a bright new song
But now it's darkened by my grief

I called her friend for just a while
Indeed it was so very true
Her gentle way made my soul smile
But now my days are often blue

Special soul right here on earth
Mortal angel, gifted one
It was that way from her birth
But her work here now is done

Yet I know she still lives on
In all those that she did touch
She dwells in Heaven with the Son
I will miss her very much

Her passing taught me all too well
To cherish each sweet joyful day
What time is left we can not tell
So make each precious moment pay

It's true I may be grieving some
But not for long a tall
Isn't good to be so glum
I will be standing tall

I will remember her so dear
And her love so warm
I know that she is ever near
And I will fear no harm

Sarah Merine

I'm a seventeen year old Haitian girl who is too young to have a voice and too old to be cared about. Writing has been a profound passion of mine just as much as reading has been. I write because penning my thoughts has become the very air I breathe.

SILENTLY IN LOVE

Eyes, deep as the Nile.
Lips, so angrily tempting.
Mind, an expansion of knowledge,
That pulls me closer than
Earth's gravitational pull.

Your smile, so coy
As your eyes crinkle.
Your laughter,
The sound of an angelic symphony.

Your words through my ears,
To my mind,
To my heart
Blood rushing, pumping
Through me.

Hands uncontrollably quivering,
Cheeks, brightening red
Flustered, unable to meet your gaze
Gasping for air whenever
You are near,
I am silently in love with you.

Blue Eyed Girl

Your dark hair caresses the small of your back
In the light of a waning moon
Darkness engulfs you
Takes you by the hand and shakes you
But your adulteress lips
Still mark my broken heart
Like eroded footprints in the sand.

Lachrymose embraces so monotonous now
While your pleas for forgiveness become
As real as your ruby red lips,
I lay alone again tonight.

Thoughts of your elegant twirls
and seductress ways remind me
of my unrequited love for you.
Your lips spew mercury, with my tongue
I swallow it whole.

Will you return? Nights like these
Make me want you more.
As my mind replays thoughts of you,
Vivid images rush in a flurry of once
deep passionate kisses and hungry collisions
of our immature love.

What happened? I lay in despair.
In desperate hope, that our love shall rekindle.
As every breath of air that fills my lungs
Reminds me of how they are wasted if I'm not with you.

My little blue eyed raven,
Will you knock, knock at my window door?
Parting glances say, nevermore.

WHEN THE PENDULUM STRIKES TWELVE

Lips quivering,
Hands all in a twist
I give you signs,
Though all you've missed.

Watching as the pendulum swings,
Slowly it taunts
For the time is approaching,
And I've flaunt all I could flaunt

My dream shatters,
My feelings deepen
Me wanting you,
My attempts cheapen
For they are worthless.

My heart throbbing,
Blood pulsing through my veins
As I wait for your kiss,
The wait driving me insane.

No way to sit still,
Once again I advance
It continues,
You, still holding your stance.

Thirty seconds remain,
Then none.
As the pendulum strikes twelve
A new day has begun.

Disappointed,
My heart paces steadily
As you finally kiss me,
We embrace, wholeheartedly.

The wait better than the event,
No fireworks explode
As I sit back in discontent.

Susan C. Cravota

Originally from Long Island, New York, my husband and I have enjoyed the Florida weather for the past fourteen years. We have two daughters and three grandchildren. I enjoy volunteering at my church, my community tap dance group, choreography, reading, writing, and dabbling in many handcrafts.

Go!

Look up through a rectangular skylight,
      and you'll see a small square of sky;
            shades of blue, white, maybe even gray or black.

Look out through a picture window,
      and you'll see a small rectangle of life:
            sky, flowers, grasses, trees, buildings, cars, animals,
                or even people.

Look through an open door,
      the portal enabling you to reach what you've seen thus far:
            imagine, dream, and wonder what really lies beyond.

Go through that portal,
      and relish the complete assault to your senses:
            myriad colors, fragrant earth, sun's heat, birdsong
            and humanity's hum.

Go and grab hold of what you find
      with all your heart and mind and all of your being;
            this is life, a treasured gift just for you to enjoy.

Go, and.........live!

THE BALLERINA

The graceful ballerina comes in through the door,
    Sits and puts her slippers on then glides across the floor.

Twirling, leaping, gliding, sweeping, all around she goes,
    Acting out the roles she plays, while dancing on her toes.

Costume changes, lace and ruffles, satins, what a sight!
    Dancing visions flashing, rainbow colors shining bright.

Soldiers and the Nutcracker dance with her 'neath the tree,
    Sugar Plum Prince spins her 'round, the world's a mystery.

Once she was a fairy queen all dressed in snowy white,
    Changing all the bad to good with magic wand so bright.

Dancing as a little maid for stepsisters so mean,
    Whirling in the prince's arms to find that she's his dream.

Spinning thread, her finger pricked, a hundred years she slept,
    Awakened by a young man's kiss, the promise had been kept.

Through the different roles she dances to the looking glass,
    While all around her students ready, "Ballerinas, begin class!"

Theresa Pavell

I'm happiest when immersed in a book and reading and writing Poetry. At present I'm working on my collection of Poetry to be titled: Poems At Random. Being a member of The Florida Writer's Association and attending Poetry readings spurs me on to write, write, write.

TOTAL RECALL

What year was that?
Please don't shrug....
Remember when
I drove a "Bug"?

What year was that?
Now, don't despair,
That happened when
I cut my hair.

What year was that?
I cannot recall.
Wasn't that when
I took a fall?

What year was that?
Now let me see....
That was the year
You married me!

LOST LOVE

Often, worried thoughts would surface.
'What would I do if we met again?'
It's a civilized world and
I've been told that I'm sophisticated.

By chance, we did meet
On a busy, crowded Street
And, we exchanged pleasant words
That meant nothing at all.

I watched as his arm
Enveloped her as they walked
Away in the opposite direction.
I felt hot tears drop

Swiftly I walked
Knowing that they could not see me.
Realization set in
I'm not sophisticated at all.

Finis.

Thomas Starr

My name is Thomas Starr. I'm 33 and live in the quaint city of DeLand, Florida. I write poetry mostly in my unique office space which doubles as our chess park. By day I'm a part time massage therapist and a full time art enthusiast.

LOVEBIRD FLU

This lovebird flu,
    In its infancy,
        Its state of new
Sentimental chirps
    Departing lips
        Falling prey upon us
Airborne, zoonotic
    Trapped in our mouths
        We bitter bystanders
Stricken with tachycardia
    Bulimia
        And Type 2 Diabetes

COMMERCIAL CAKE SALES

Candied Caspers carried
Among chocolate dreams
Dancing in commercials
Coating their hidden schemes

This cake has dried out
In bitterness of air
Moisture evaporates
From texture's harden stare

I'm a diabetic,
Overindulgent tooth
Biting your bitter bars
Saturated in youth

Twinkle Marie Manning

"Twinkle" Marie Manning is originally from Boston and has lived many places including New Smyrna Beach, Florida. She is an artist, writer, TV and radio host and producer. Her poems speak to us about moments in our lives which lift us above the ordinary. She is a mother to four beautiful children: Dylan, Morgan, Riley and Orion.

OUR DANCE

Swept away by the music
Each note gives rise to higher sensation

That soft moment between the notes
The undulation of our breath, still
Heat alive in our eyes

Every movement sends us
spiraling toward each other
Embracing my heart,
tugging remembrance from my soul

You are here

You are here

Our dance continues.

OUR CONGREGATION GATHERS

Dawn breaks slowly here
Ocean lapping at the shore
Lovingly leisure
I rise from my rest filled slumber
Don my headset
And run to the beach

I dance
I twirl
I skip through the waves lapping at the shore
The sand a delight
Beneath my bare feet

Alone yet surrounded by
Other early risers
Dancing their dance
As they worship Sunrise with me
I pause to truly take in my surroundings
I see with great fondness and appreciation
The entire congregation is here this morning

The seagulls
The sandpipers
The tiny sand fleas they feast upon as the water rushes home
to the Sea
Oh look, the joggers appear; they are always running behind
Tai Chi to the right
Surfers heading left towards the Inlet

The ocean whirls for me as I jump in the water
Round and round my dancing spin
Stop
Breathe
Smile
A glance back to our God rising out of the Atlantic
And, there, in the near distance — dolphins
Dancing along with me.

Thank you and Namaste.

Wendy Thornton

Wendy Thornton has published poetry, fiction and non-fiction in such journals as Epiphany, MacGuffin, Main Street Rag, Literary Review, Riverteeth, etc. She was nominated for a Pushcart Prize and was a finalist for the Glimmer Train short fiction prize. She has been selected as an Editor's Pick multiple times on salon.com and is President of the Writers Alliance of Gainesville.

IF I KNEW HOW

If I knew how to get back
I'd follow that Yellow Brick Road
and undrop the house I dumped on your sister.

If I knew how to get back
I'd reverse those engines,
scrap that lunar landing
and glowing float slowly down to earth.

If I knew how to get back
I'd drop that ring into the void
and bound in after it, giving up the quest.

If I knew how to get back
I'd reverse the tether,
unfold time and call for a redo.

If only I knew how much I'd miss you
I'd get back.
Send directions.

THIS IS THE SOUND

of two sticks rubbing together –
smoking because I turned him down
too much a man to say that hurt,
still he plans to make me work
make me beg, make me want
all the essence of regret, all reluctance gone.

Hold that glass to a flat dry leaf,
grab the flint and strike that steel.
Make sparks fly, make me feel,
make me remember why we're here,
To be warm to be near to touch to flirt —
Come on baby, you call this work?

APPASSIONATO

What can I do to show you
how much you have done for me
how much your world rocks me
how wild my world wants you
how wide my eyes widen
how wide the path I walk on
the path you built for me
that brick by brick supports me
built that path to cavort with me
built that path to lift me
a fort we enter together
man of my dreams
I didn't know I was dreaming.
Used to think I wanted a blond — boy
was I off the mark
you so dark.

Janet Redemann Sage

Janet Redemann Sage is an author and scholar who has taught at the high school and college level. Her career as a writer, teacher and scholar spans the Atlantic to England, where she had associations, while at Oxford, with Albert Finney, and with the Moody Blues. She is the author of the acclaimed poetry collection, *Rise Above*. She resides in South Daytona.

TELL ME

Who inspired the angels to sing?
In the deep - valleyed voice of green joys
Awakening from a dream, there must have
Been someone more beautiful
Or something great, sweet, and large - or larger -
Than the breath of Spring.

But, when did one below
Behold the Beautiful of a perfect
Light and, with painful eyes, shudder and
Deny the stars? What kept him
From rejoicing — when to be
Alive was such a simple thing.

You Are Asleep

You are asleep, beautiful soul;
On this first day of the year,
You lie tranquil and shining,
Like this silent morning.
Counter-part to you, I toss violently
In restless thought, till down from peace,
I press my nose against our window:
Sudden cold and snow descended through the night;
Now trees lean in the ice-bound frames,
Glorious and welcome to my sight;
They tempt me now to join the winter air and sun,
And I leave you, my beautiful one,
To journey in remembrance of your light.

I step quickly in my high-laced boots
Careful not to break apart what seems
To be less restless; yet I discover soon
The lightest touch yielding pressure;
Down closer to those roots
And yearning, slow and stretching long,
Long and gentle, snow-awakening,
Now the January of the year.

Is it not true (we have murmured once before)
that even rude winds must yield at last to calm?
Carrying in its ravage, seeds deep sigh,
Laboring long, the wind must die,
Scattering to distant parts what it seemed to steal away.

The whole earth rises.
And the craft of death's second, longer still:
March rains, April laughter, May beginning the multiple

> harvest, crocus, blackberry and apple
Blossom, dogwood, tulip and cherry, passionate
Azalea, the rose; bright and vital corn and cucumber,
> Summer melons, the sunflower,
Tiger lilies, gladiolas; ripe pear and plum,
And in each season mellow, cold, and warm,
and now the pumpkin,
Asters, leaves; the laurel,
> And now the January of the year.

Now returning after those rude thoughts
Of leaving, I die again before you;
And I whisper, richly fashioned,
Offering all received this day:
Sweet sleep, the lull of waking in thy way.

Rapture

To capture the moment of stillness
    around you and let it glide
Over the peaceful waters of your wondering
    how deeply you feel inside -
It is the miracle of your wonder,
    let it grow, let it grow,
For an age can be beginning,
    it's everything you sow
From the now, from the moment
    of your stillness reaching out
To tell the world of its wonder
    (if it knew what it's about).

Open up, you are coming
    to an age of love and peace,
If you feel you are winning
    when you give the word release

Quiet, how quiet it all is
    down
        the hills
Of white thunder I am running for the sun
to be near the endless wonder
Of my loved and loving one

    Soul in the rapture of the music he is making,
        every breath he is taking.

Rob Dunning

Rob Dunning is a prolific poet who generates new poems almost daily. A former Merchant Marine sailor, he has published numerous collections of his poetry, including *Small Voodoo, Imperfect Eyes, Auditory Hallucinations,* and his latest book, *Heroes and Pirates Poems.* He lives and works in New Smyrna Beach, where he is renowned as a legend of the underground .

CERTAIN

Let's sandblast our arrogant sins at this moment.
Brightly-lit salvation is simple.
The concentrated headlights of an elegant roadster
Cruises on the Boulevard.
Cleansing rainfall washes away angry insults and scattered
Fighting from a tortured furious hill.
Today I might be gone but I know everything like a smooth
Blue whale
Diving toward accessible distance in the sunny South
Atlantic.
The waiting world is still round and the beachhead laughs
With the assisting wind.

Find breathing space on the continent.
Let's keep the horribly wrong somewhere broke down.
Embrace the real mystery.
Find the agreeable circumstances of our useful lives.

Beneath a Graffiti Moon

Don't let me forget the derelicts on dope,
Old men sleeping beside public urinals,
And the grimacing bag-ladies
Tattooed with inscrutable riddles of sweltering
Injustices
Emerging like stowaways on rudderless ships
Amid the shivering streets and concrete alleyways
In the middle of the night downtown.

Poets of Central Florida

MORE OR LESS

On the shifting sand
I feel sadness
Or the rain approaching.
How can we breathe so lonely?
A boat quickens
To a swell thickening without color.
In front of it a faded gull flies alone.
My mind floats away
Through the half-buried sunset,
All its scars crossed by bird tracks.

165

Karen Kershaw

I am a Poet and Performance Artist of words. My craft of choice is X-tra fine black tip pen upon paper, performing upon request and even when not requested, in inspired moments. I love to shine and I love to share that shine. I perform words with passion. Illuminated letters light my way to a written piece, Illuminated presence ,embodies them. Read or watch/listen/experience my story, and let me share my brilliance with you.

RHAPSODY OF EVE

light descends

blush on the cheek of the soon to be night

snake light tendrils, slither to the bush,
caressing, then, leaves

a day it's end, for men and women

quieter in the cooling garden,
buds, pulse, closing

eve takes hold, wraps her arms, tight,
slowly
          ride her down to midnight

SOMETIMES THE SUN....

Some times the sun she hid under the stair
she could see who comes and goes from there
under the stair
she dared
repose
not shine so brightly
tease passerby's, who go by, not so lightly
she let off a little light they come closer
she let out a little warmth from under
with all her might
she tucked her bright
brilliance
tempered by the steps at night
hot stuff kept in a cool dark place
she's hot stuff kept in a cool dark place
shone
rays
shine on for days
off in the night
 she slipped under
 the light
sometimes the sun, she hid under the stair

CINQUAIN SHE MOVED

    moved
she tripped light-ly down the avenue
      beat in her head drove her forward
    hold up

    turned
catch her watching herself plate glass windows
it up smiles behind, watch her
    go 'round

    stopped
the scene she made
down on the avenue caused gasps and public displays
      don't move

      stretched
beyond repair
her fragile self aware once more shameful disrepair crazy
      broken

      open
to the cop car picks her up takes her far
hardly ... home, a cool suite ... unit 3
    shut up

Rosemary Volz

Rosemary Volz was born in Brooklyn, New York and attended Queens College where she graduated summa cum laude with a double major in Creative Writing and Journalism. She has won numerous literary awards. Her short stories and poetry have appeared in Blueline, Event, Another Chicago Magazine and Reader's Choice. She has four children and four grandchildren and now lives in Ponce Inlet with her husband Jim.

I Do Not Love with Abandon

I do not love with abandon.
I do not vault, run or catapult.
I come to the sheets lumbering,
Clumsy in my love.
I bring childhood fears,
Unpaid bills, a lost book,
God the father and his star-crossed Son,
Guilt by association,
Cruelty by procrastination,
A body ripe with betrayal,
A soul lost and found and lost again.

> I cannot touch the wound without becoming
> the wound.
> I cannot greet the darkness without becoming
> the darkness.

I bring Lucy and Ricky, Ozzie and Harriet,
John and Abigail,
A broken promise,
A No. 2 pencil,
The tin plate beneath the cat's dish

A peasant in her queen-sized bed
Turning awkwardly
Toward a promise of oblivion.

MARILYN

I was a teenager when she died,
Only beginning to understand
The exchange rate of a tight sweater,
A careless toss of the hair,
A playful swing of the hips.

I saw the photo of her on a stretcher
Being carried out of a sad-looking house;
A house where the cat's dish is always empty,
A house that flies the flag of nowhere.
Her head tossed back, skin discolored,
Beyond the reach of God and DiMaggio,
More beautiful than ever.

I wondered about that night
When the lemony dusk disappeared
And the sky crashed down on her
Casting its relentless shadows
On those perfect thighs,
On those perfect breasts,
On that perfect face.
She is gripping the edge of the bed;
She is gripping the edge of eternity,
But here is nothing left to keep her
Locked to this world.
There is no center.
There is no past or future,
Only an unbearable urge to spin and shine.
So crashing against the earth's crust,
She splinters into a million sparkly pieces.
No one can stand the light.
No one can save her.

For a moment we ponder
Self and sex,

170

Body and soul,
But at the end
All this titillated world remembers
Is a white dress
Billowing above a subway gate.

WONDER

I woke up this morning and the
Gold and purple tree from
Last night's dream was
Blooming on my front lawn.

I ran for the train and
My right knee didn't hurt at all.
It was 8:22 and the 8:15 Express
Was waiting for me.

I reached into my pocket for the ticket
And found my lost keys and a gold doubloon.
A window seat was empty and
A copy of tomorrow's paper was left behind.

The conductor handed me a cup of coffee
And a silver bowl filled with grapes,
So I sat back and watched
Seven corpulent angels cavorting on clouds.

The day was uneventful until I came home
And wonders of wonders,
You were there,
Waiting
Smiling.

Niki Byram

Niki Byram received her B.A. in biology from St. Mary's College in Maryland, which led her to a career as a Histotechnologist. She is married and lives in Daytona Beach. She has always wanted to find outlets for her creativity and is currently writing poetry, taking art classes, and enjoys taking photographs from her kayak.

LATER

Last night I held you and
You fell asleep in my arms.
You fit me perfectly.

To be truthful, last night
You held me and I fell
Asleep in your arms.

Did I fit you?

So long in coming, I've always
Wanted you and this...a love beginning...

If we spoke, I don't recall a word;
Just getting comfortable with how we
Fit together was a monumental event.

The holding was what was needed to
Establish and build trust.

We can talk later,
We can touch later,
We can kiss later,
We can make love later,
Because now we both sense and know,
There will be a later.

Love Is....You

Love is your smile, that crinkles up the corners of your eyes,
Giving me a deep and silent heartfelt welcome.

Love is the softness of your hand as we touch,
With promises of more touching to come.

Love is your dreamy expression,
As I hold the face I love between the
Palms of my hands.

Love is the trusting assent your eyes give me
As I lean toward you for a kiss.

Love is feeling your warm breath on my neck
As you snuggle into my hug.

Love is the way your head feels, cupped in my hand,
As I hold you in my embrace waiting to catch
Another breath against my skin.

Love is knowing that we can love like this,
Over and over again.

Love is one word...YOU.

Carol Thomas

Dr. Carol Thomas holds a Ph.D. in Literature and Psychology, a doctorate in Applied Theology, a Master of Art's Degree in English Literature from Stetson University, and a Master's Degree in Counseling Psychology. She has taught Literature, Psychology, and Women's Studies at various Colleges and Universities, and Creative Writing for Saint Leo University and Gavle University in Storvik, Sweden.

Prairie Home Companion

I love the prairie like you might love
a friend, a lover, a book you've read a

hundred times or more; eight years of
outdoor life, the "I" of me shrunk down

to new humility, and yet expanded in each
moment; last week anxiety and shame took

off, regret left too, ran after them, and then
internal censor, banging on my door, stopped

her nattering and left; my clunky, jittery, self
began to dance in rain and sun; some days I

ride my horse ten miles, pet my dog and read; some
days I dream, pick flowers, bake an apple pie, or think;

I threw away my phone, my shoes, my keys; forked,
unaccommodated creature, woman, the prairie
called me home to stay

FIREFLIES
AFTER LEONARD COHEN

we sit outside as twilight comes, mist covering new
sprouts of winter wheat, tired geraniums in dusky light

   then fireflies spark out between the old world blue
and sunflower skeletons as though just anything deserved

these tiny miracles of lights, phosphorescent blings; you show
me how to find the moons of Jupiter, orbits, constellations,

hard to find with untrained eye; I ask you to define an orbit
of the moon, you try to tell a mind unscientific, you give

me theories of the sky and a lesson in physics, then about
discoveries Galileo made, and how orbits are elliptical;

I try to listen but I am swooning at the blazing light
of twinkling upside down earth stars and I see *the crack,*

the crack in everything that lets the light come in, but I am
so drunk, inebriated with the little blinking lights the

beauty of the light, I cannot speak, I can hear no sound;
   mesmerized, hypnotized, no longer on the earth

MIRACLE
FOR LEONARD COHEN

so much depends on green imagination,
rain, red dirt, bluestem, how things root and grow,

each strand of living matter poised, positioned as
only it can be; we can train ourselves to live without

love, wine, justice, sex, or company; we can live without
consoling nonsense of sky fathers there to pick

us up perpetually; we cannot live without new metaphors
of body, breast, song, holding, touching skin to skin;

today cold hard winter's knuckles dapple air, stars
signal grace to ordinary hearts, *waiting for the*

miracle to come is now, near this warm fire, a roof,
wood by the door, a body's willingness to share its heat

to warm another body with its holding power,
unconditional, requited

Phyllis L. Lober

Phyllis Lober is an educator listed in Who's Who in Education. She holds a Masters Degree and Doctorate in Educational Studies. During her long career she received many awards, including the Fulbright Fellowship from Columbia University. She was invited to teach in the People's Republic of China, where she co-authored *The Teaching of English Skills*, a text for Chinese teachers.

THE LILT OF THE LUTE

(A CHINESE PHENOMENON)

I wander through time and space,
cast adrift in the human race.
No longer in my room dreaming,
but rather lost in reverie sleeping.
It came to me as I drifted toward clouds on high
listening to the ballet both soft and dry,
casting nets of silver and gold into my dreams of
boys and girls
from opera and ballet of "The Butterfly Lovers,"
came the elegance of white pearls.

The night was softly swaying
and I, thinking of children playing.
Suddenly, came the harsh sounds of cement pouring
into a thunderous cavern pounding
into my head, my ears, my body.

I was drowning in cement to build their apartments all ready.
Time took my night at one a.m. in the morning,
leaving me drained and soaring
into the horror of the sound
making my head and body parts pound.

By daybreak, at six a.m. still drained by the pouring
of cement,
there came the beauty of the lilt of the lute so dominant
in my mind; wearing an apron the color of blue,   (*cont.*)

177

like a jaybird worn,
and jeans frazzled, blue and ripped and torn,
hair black as night, eyes dewy brown and jacket red as a
butterfly.
In his mouth a handmade flue with incredible musical sound,
wafting high into the sky.

I listened as the early morning scene lifted itself
into the air.
At the window watching and listening,
adoring with a juvenile dare.
The horror of the night had disappeared from view.
Only the music of the flute player stayed at my door.
It was Saturday morning, no school for a lost soul.
Only the music of the flute player remained in my bowl.

He lifted me to never land, playing "the Butterfly lovers,"
and I thought of Chinese boys and girls, lost in dreams
of doers.
It was a happy day for me,
the past brought me to the present, and I see.

John E. Lunievicz

John Lunievicz is the deceased son of Phyllis Lober of Port Orange, Florida. He was a talented young musician and writer. Following his sudden and violent departure from this world, a collection of his poems was discovered by his mother. The poem presented here is part of that previously unpublished collection.

SOLITUDE

Solitude, hold me in your sweet arms,
forever and forever.
Let me slumber, let me dream
of dawn's fingers bright and orange.
Let me be dawn.

Solitude, let me step through a
cloud, the mountain fresh air, and
dance to the funny man with his
lute and his dreams.

Hold me in your beauty, shine within and without;
cleanse my wounds when they hurt.

Solitude, lead me to an open
field, there to taste the autumn,
and dream of the spring.

Let me feel nature with
images I can't understand. Hold me
peace, forever and forever.

Solitude, I love you.

CPSIA information can be obtained at www.ICGtesting.com
Printed in the USA
LVOW110041220212

269841LV00005B/1/P